Praise for <u>You Are 1</u>

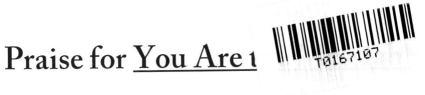

Why do you keep mailing your confusing manuscript to our offices? We have no interest in publishing this kind of material. Please kindly also stop sending semi-nude pictures of yourself, as there is no chance of you becoming a part of our company's talent roster.

- World Universal Wrestling Magazine

Well, this certainly is a book, isn't it? Front and back covers, and in between those there are lots of pages that are filled with words. It's made of paper. That is about all I am comfortable saying about it.

- Name withheld upon request, famous book reviewer

Let me guess. You're going to stick a quote from me in the front of your book, nestled in between a few other fake quotes from nonexistent people/publications...Real original, asshole.

- Chris Trew, friend of the author

Meh.

- Internet, universal electronic information resource

This is a hilarious book. Why oh why did we treat you like such a dorky loser all those years ago? We're so sorry. Please forgive us.

- What all the people who went to high school with the author should say now

Also by Brock LaBorde:

The Semi-Complete Guide to Sort of Being a Gentleman

YOU ARE THE MESSIAH!

BY BROCK LABORDE

ILLUSTRATED BY CARLA A. TOME

Another great book from Studio8.net!

You Are the Messiah!
Choose-A-Choice Book #1

iUniverse books may be ordered through booksellers or by contacting:

iUniverse
1663 Liberty Drive
Bloomington, IN 47403
www.iuniverse.com
1-800-Authors (1-800-288-4677)

ISBN: 978-1-4502-6896-7 (pbk)
ISBN: 978-1-4502-6898-1 (cloth)
ISBN: 978-1-4502-6897-4 (ebk)

Printed in the United States of America

iUniverse rev. date: 1/8/11

This book is dedicated to Jesus Christ, whose mere existence is solely responsible for this book's relevance.

It is also dedicated to you, the reader, because you (hopefully) paid for this book with money of some sort and I <u>really</u> love me some money.

Palestine
(30-something A.D.)

edge of the world

Mediterranean Sea

edge of the world

edge of the world

caeserea Philippi

Sand And Rocks

capernaum

Magdala

Nazareth

Galilee

Sea of galilee

caesarea

Gadarenes

Samaria

Unexplored Wilderness

River Jordan

golgotha

garden of gethsemene

Jerusalem   Jericho

Bethany
    Bethlehem

Judaea

Wide Open Space

WASTELAND

The DEAD Sea

The Dead LAKE

Dust Bowl

THE DEAD POND

THE DEAD RIVER

THE DEAD BAYOU

Nothing at All

edge of the world

WARNING!!!

This book, being a ridiculous work of complete fiction, is just about as factually accurate as our modern Bible, which is pretty scary if you think about it. It's also not a normal book, in the sense that you start at the first page and read consecutive pages until the story's over. Instead, you'll have to put some effort into this if it's going to work—making choices about where you want the narrative to go and turning to the appropriate page numbers. But be careful! For along the way, you'll run into a lot of different endings to this story—some good, most bad.

Once you turn this page, you will become the man widely known as Jesus Christ of Nazareth and you'll get to make all the decisions in his short, oh-so-blessed life. The story unfolds in the time period of the New Testament Gospels (30-ish AD). You'll visit all of the places that the Bible says Jesus hung around and you'll get to meet all of the weirdos who Jesus encountered. But you'll also find many things/characters/scenarios that weren't in the Bible because, despite its mind-numbingly monstrous girth, the Bible's authors somehow managed to leave out a lot of fun stuff.

If you're at all familiar with biblical folklore and stories, you should be able to make the right choices to earn the best ending, although many of the traditional "right" choices will have very different outcomes than you'd expect. So maybe you're better off having no biblical knowledge at all. Eh, you're kind of screwed no matter who you are or what you do.

One thing's for sure, though—you're about to set out on a really swell journey of spiritual discovery. And since you'll be sporting the sandals of the flesh-and-blood Son of the Almighty God, your story won't always necessarily end when you die. As the Bible itself can testify, a great many things can happen beyond mortal death…

One more thing! To anyone who finds something offensive in the language, situations, or the overall concept and existence of this book, <u>chill out</u>! It's a make-believe story written by a weird, imperfect, semi-educated dude trying to make some sense of this crazy world in which we all must live—a dude just like the dudes who wrote the Bible so long ago.

This book, just like the Bible, is strictly for entertainment purposes…

A knock on the curtain of your hut jolts you out of a strange dream.

With half-opened eyes, you grumble for your parents, Mary and Joseph, to answer the door.

When the knocking starts up again, you remember that today is the day that your parents were taking your younger brothers and sisters to watch a group of harlots get stoned to death.

You've got the whole day to yourself!

You jump up from your bed of dust and rocks and take three steps forward—passing through the living room, kitchen, dining room, kitchenette, and foyer—to the front door of your family's tiny hut.

Pulling back the door curtain, you see your best friend, Simon Peter Timothy, excitedly jumping up and down.

"Jesus, Jesus!"

He's yelling and pulling your arm.

"Put on your swimming robe and let's get going! We've really got to hoof it if we're going to make it to the River Jordan by noon!"

That's right! You forgot that you had planned to go on a double-date with Simon Peter Timothy and a couple of girls at the river today.

You change out of your sleeping robe, throw on your sandals, and head out the door.

Before you leave, you scribble a note on some papyrus for your parents in case they return before you do.

It reads:

"Gone fig hunting. Fear ye not, for I shall return very soon.

Love,
JC"

Turn to the NEXT PAGE

2

"Are we really going on a date? Like, *with girls?* My parents would totally crucify me if they knew we were doing this," you tell Simon Peter Timothy as the two of you begin the long trek across town.

"Jesus, you're thirty-two years old," he replies. "You're not some little baby boy away in a manger anymore. Besides, it might really be worth getting in trouble over. I heard that your date, Mary, flashed her bare shoulder to some boys behind the youth synagogue last week."

For a moment, you fantasize about Mary's naked shoulder hanging out for all the world to see, but soon your thoughts drift back to the time your parents caught you preaching in the temple when you were a teenager. They sure were sore about it, and you don't want to disappoint them like that again.

Gee, that seems like so long ago, you wonder.

And indeed it was, roughly 20 years. Oddly enough, you can't remember much else that's happened in your life, either before or after that day. It's like you were a baby one day and then a teenager the next, and now you're suddenly a middle-aged man.

Regardless, you're pretty certain that you haven't preached anywhere ever since that day when you were twelve.

Lately, though, you've been having these weird dreams that you were a preacher, and a darn famous one at that...

Simon Peter Timothy slugs you in the arm. "Don't worry about what your stuffy-ass parents say, Jesus. You're so naïve! You honestly believe that your parents were virgins when they were your age?"

"My mom definitely was. I think she still is," you say.

"You'll be fine. You need to live a little, dude."

He's right. But then again, Simon Peter Timothy has a knack for making you ignore your responsibilities, which is one reason why your parents don't like you hanging out with him.

Another reason is that he's a filthy Gentile and you're Jewish.

You relax and the two of you continue on your way.

Later, you are both thirsty and exhausted from the intense mid-day heat and from swatting at the swarms of flies and gnats that follow everyone around all the time.

"Sheesh! Are we having another insect plague or what?" Simon Peter Timothy asks, frustrated.

"Maybe people are falling behind on their sacrifices to Jehovah," you offer.

As you approach the river, you notice that it's a lot more populated than it usually would be on a day like this. A crowd is gathered along both sides of the riverbank, watching a man who shouts and splashes about in the waist-deep water.

"Aw cripes! That John the Baptist dude is out here baptizing people again," Simon Peter Timothy laments. "He's absolutely bat-shit crazy about baptisms."

You scan the dense crowd, but don't see any sign of your dates, so the two of you decide to watch John the Baptist scream and dunk people's heads underwater for a while.

As Simon Peter Timothy looks for a good seat on the muddy bank, you walk down to the river's edge for a quick sip of water.

"Hey there! You with the beard, robe, and sandals!" a voice shouts.

Every man in attendance (including you) starts looking around, pointing at themselves, and asking aloud, "Who? Me?"

"Yeah you!" the voice answers.

Finally you follow the voice to its source and see that it's John the Baptist and he's pointing right at you, a crazed look in his eyes.

"You look like you're in need of a real good baptizing, yessir!" he screams. "So get your filthy, un-baptized self out here and let me baptize you!"

Ugh! How mortifying! It feels like everyone in the world is staring at you right now.

Turn to PAGE 8

4

You arrive at the wedding just in time to see your mother, Mary, and your sister, Mary, busily braiding some baskets as last-minute wedding gifts. Feeling like you're not yet ready to confront them and defend your recent Messianic expedition, you attempt to duck out of their line of sight.

Just then, a man waves and calls out from across the pavilion, "Hey, Jesus!"

You freeze and attempt to signal the man to shut up, but he doesn't get it.

"Thanks so much for healing my lame brother," he says in an even louder voice. "Man, he was the lamest dude ever before you came along!"

Hearing this, your mother looks up and immediately spots you. Throwing her basket down, she charges at you and pinches your ear so hard that she almost tears it off.

"Jesus Theodore Christ! You have quite some bit of explaining to do, young man!" she bellows. "You don't come home for months and I hear you're performing miracles all over town? What, you couldn't find the time to turn some trees into hundreds of collectible cat statues to help out your poor father who's breaking his back with all his carpentering? And what's with all this preaching? Who taught you how to sermonize like that?"

"Ma, hold on. It's not so easy to explain," you whine. "You'd probably need a ridiculously thick, confusing book and half a million derivative self-help books to even begin to understand whatever ministry it is that I've started here."

Before she can respond, someone announces that it's time for the wedding couple to make their big wedding toast.

Everyone falls respectfully silent as the young bride and groom say a few cute words to one another and then clink their goblets.

However, their clinks sound more like hollow thuds, and when they take their sips, they find there's no wine in their goblets.

"We're all out of wine!" the bride screams, glaring at the groom before storming off into the honeymoon hut and repeatedly attempting to slam the curtain shut.

The wedding planner drags a few jugs of water out of a house.

"Oh God! There's been some sort of mix-up. Somebody accidentally watered the camels with all of the wine!"

So that explains why the camels started brawling, having sex, and then crashed out of their pens a little while ago, you think.

"I'm afraid that these jugs of water are all we've got to drink," he says, obviously embarrassed.

You feel a slight tingle in your fingertips. Your disciples look at you. Your mother shakes her head. You eye the water jugs.

"Well, perhaps I can be of service," you meekly suggest.

Everyone turns to you.

"Oh sure, you can just magically turn water into wine just like that, Jesus," Thomas says with a snicker. "You're better off taking those useless coca leaves and that sugar cane over there and dumping that in the water!"

"Helping the underprivileged is one thing, Jesus, but performing off-the-cuff parlor tricks involving alcoholic beverages is quite another," your mother says, her eyes narrowing.

You look to your sister Mary, but she just tsk-tsks you and makes you feel even more like a loser.

And what's with Thomas? His doubtful outlook is starting to be a real bummer.

Should you prove him wrong by changing the water into wine? Or is there something to his crazy coca leaf idea? It seems like something worth pursuing.

You don't want to further disappoint your mother by using your limitless supernatural powers in a silly way, but these poor people don't want to toast with mere water on their special day...

Do something, Jesus!

If you turn the water into wine, turn to PAGE 38

If you use the coca leaves, turn to PAGE 122

6

Ok, time to put my miracle-making ass to the test, you think.

You take one of the fish, tear off a wedge of bread, and hold them both up to Heaven. You mumble some serious-sounding gibberish and then put the food up to your mouth.

"Num-num-num-num," you say, pretending to eat the fish and bread. You belch loudly, then rub your belly and wipe your forehead as if you can't eat anymore.

At first, the people stare at you, confused. Your disciples quickly start mimicking your actions and handing out little pieces of the food.

The crowd catches on, and eventually everyone follows suit, pretending to eat and passing the tidbits of fish and bread around.

For the next hour, the air hums with smacks, burps, and people repeating, "Num-num-num-num."

Your trick worked! Soon enough, all four thousand people are satisfied, their still-empty stomachs thoroughly fooled by their even emptier skulls.

"Nice one, Jesus," says Simon Peter, nodding toward a ship anchored nearby. "But I think we should make a hasty exit, real quick and fast-like, because your little ruse might not last for very long."

You agree with this tidbit of wisdom and sneak over to the boat.

The captain tells you that they're headed for Magdala and if you agree to heal all of his crew's scurvy, he'll let you ride along.

Scurvy? Ha! That doesn't stand a chance against your healing powers, so off you go!

When you get to the shore of Magdala, you realize that not only have the four thousand people figured out your fake food miracle, but they were also somehow able to anticipate your ship's course. And now they're even hungrier and have somehow added a thousand more starving people to their ranks.

Gulp!

"Hey there, everyone," you anxiously greet them. "Somehow I must've gotten turned around and lost you before I could feed you a proper meal, you large multitude of ravenous people, you..."

They aren't laughing. You start to really sweat.

"Uh, how about I heal some of your sicklies?" you offer.

You nervously touch a couple of Siamese twin children and separate them into a pair of healthy, normal children.

The crowd isn't taking that bait, though. They just want some calories...and fast.

You huddle up your disciples and ask for whatever food they've got stashed away.

They manage to scrounge together five loaves of moldy bread and two rotten fish, less than what you had before.

Great.

Those Siamese kids just gave you an idea, though.

Maybe you could try splitting the bread and fish enough times to feed all five thousand people.

However, that's kind of a weird miracle to pull off and if you fail at it, well, even if you escape with your life, you'll make thousands of new enemies and you might as well kiss your ministry goodbye.

Since this situation is headed for disaster anyway, you've had a really cool Last Supper speech kicking around in your head that you could try out. You were saving it up to be sort of a poignant, sentimental way to say goodbye to your disciples in case you ever felt like someone was about to persecute you and kill you.

It's timely and food-related, if nothing else, you think.

You've got to try something, though. What to do, what to do...

If you feed the five thousand, turn to PAGE 87

If you serve them the Last Supper, turn to PAGE 108

8

You don't like the idea of taking a dip with this freaky-looking guy in front of all these strangers. He's wearing a smelly old camel skin vest and there's an oil slick floating around him in the water.

Plus, you've heard stories about how he eats uncooked worms and rubs wild honey on his head to attract bees to live in his hair.

You glance back at Simon Peter Timothy and he gives you two thumbs up and a knowing smile that says, "You have to do this."

Others in the crowd urge you to go on, too, and even though you have no reason to listen to the unwarranted advisements of a bunch of strangers, you kick off your sandals and slowly wade into the river.

"You know what, John, I think my parents already baptized me when I was a baby. But I don't really remember," you nervously mumble.

"Just keep coming to me, O Unwashed One," he says.

As you draw closer to John, he recoils and begins jerking about spastically.

"Oh! I knew it! It's you," he shouts. "The Messiah! My Savior!"

"What?" you say, looking around. "Uh, you must have me confused with somebody else."

"No, it's you, Jesus! I'm not worthy!"

"How do you know my name?" you ask. "You're starting to creep me out, guy."

"Because you are the one true Son of God," he cries. "I've been prophesying about your arrival for months. And now, finally, *you* have come to baptize *me*!"

The crowd gasps at this. You stand crotch-deep in the dirty water, feeling awkward and not sure how to react.

He wants you to baptize him now? If you do that, it will be the talk of the town for weeks and your parents will surely find out about it. But if you don't do it, everyone might think you're a total wiener.

Either way, you're already out here, marinating in this funky dude's bodily fluids, and that double-date is looking less and less like a possibility at this point.

If you baptize John first, turn to PAGE 14

If you decline and insist that John baptize you, turn to PAGE 46

10

"All right, Zach," you tell him. "I don't know why you're up in that tree, why I should trust you, or how everyone seems to know more about my tax liabilities than I do, but I'll go to your house if it means you can get me out of this stupid mess."

"Awesome," he says, jumping out of the tree. "I'm the best damn CPA in town. You won't regret this, I swear! Follow me."

Everyone (including the priests, random townsfolk, and a few beasts of burden) follows Zaccheus to his house. Practically the whole town crams into the room and watches over your shoulder as Zaccheus prepares your taxes.

Hours later, when every last cent is accounted for, the ledger reveals that your financial situation is worse than the Pharisees thought—you've never paid taxes before and you actually owe half a million shekels to the Roman government.

You'll never be able to pay that off!

You slowly turn and address the crowd of angry faces.

"Whaaaaat?" you say. "Don't blame me. I've been living with my parents. They handle all that kind of stuff."

The people are not amused, even after you cure Zaccheus's wife's crooked spine and his son's harelip, which is why he wanted you to visit his house in the first place.

Within minutes, the high priests have alerted the Roman authorities and you are arrested and imprisoned for tax fraud, tax evasion, and general unpatriotic and suspicious behaviors.

"You were wrong, Zach. I totally regret this," you sadly tell Zaccheus before they drag you off.

Months later, you are beheaded, suffering the death of a common white-collar criminal.

As your head rolls away from your body, before everything goes black, you glimpse all of your blood gushing out of your neck and into the dirt, a waste of perfectly good Messianic sin-cleansing blood.

What a pitiful pity.

THE END

Against your better judgment, you decide to continue the healing spree.

"All right. Just this one more thing and then I'm done for the day," you announce, which is met with a groan from the endlessly diseased crowd.

You reach down and touch the tortured pile of flesh at your feet. Immediately, she unfolds herself, stands tall, and resembles a happy, healthy woman.

"Thank you, Jesus," she says, looking around bewildered. "I am made whole!"

Her husband cries and shakes your hand. Several ladies swoon. Children proudly lift homemade Jesus dolls into the air. It is a fine moment.

Later, outside of town, you ask your disciples what ailment they think that poor woman suffered from.

"Demonic possession," says Matthew. "I asked her neighbor. I have the whole thing transcribed."

"It was definitely rickets," says Simon Peter. "My assistant Mark wrote down rickets in his book."

"Woman? What woman?" asks Simon. "I wasn't paying attention. I was busy writing this story called 'Luke' about Jesus."

"It doesn't matter what sickness she had as long as Jesus was the one healing her," says John. "That's an excerpt from my forthcoming diary entry about today. I write in my special Jesus Journal every day."

You look at the four men quizzically.

"Wait a minute. All four of you are separately documenting our journey and my teachings?"

"Yeah, but I miss some stuff here and there," Matthew admits.

"Mark has assured me that our version of things is utterly infallible," Simon Peter beams.

"I just get all the juicy stuff, the action, the sex-" Simon starts.

"Excuse me, sir," you interrupt him. "But what's your name again? Are you one of my disciples?"

"I'm Simon. I signed up with you back in Galilee."

"Oh. I just don't remember you," you say warily. "I should assign all of you guys numbers or something."

"Well, I listed all twelve of us out in my diary, Jesus, so don't you worry about that," says John. "Of course, I'm at the top of the list since you love me the most."

Turn to the NEXT PAGE

12

"Uh huh," you say. "I'm just worried about all four of you writing down vastly different things. What if they somehow get published and people start comparing the four accounts and they don't match up? That could be quite controversial and perhaps even detrimental to the integrity of my teachings."

"Je-zoo, buddy…controversy is our friend," Bartholomew pipes in. "It gets people talking, questioning things. The more questions they have, the more they look to you for answers. Plus, having four guys writing all of this stuff down, that's just more exposure for you. All press is good press. And as of now it's all free, baby!"

He makes a good point. Damn, that Bartholomew is one persuasive dude.

"Well, let me just officially go on record and say that I don't ever want the accounts of Matthew, Mark, Luke, and John compiled together into one single book, ok? It's too risky and confusing and I'm scared that too many dishonest, opportunistic people might take advantage of the errors and discredit all my teachings in the future."

"Duly noted!" the four exclaim as they pretend to write that down.

The thirteen of you continue on your way.

Turn to PAGE 35

Who do these Pharisee jerks think they are? You're the Alpha and Omega, the Beginning *and* the End, Jehovah Jirah, Jehovah Nissi, and many other fancy Hebrew words!

And you're about to give them a sign they won't forget.

"Mortis Kalamata Chimichanga…" you ramble on in your deepest voice, which honestly isn't all that deep. You roll your eyes back in your skull and spread out your arms.

The crowd cowers in anticipation.

BWACK-THOOM! A huge crack opens up in the ground and a gigantic, hairy pair of human butt-cheeks slowly rises out of the depths.

"It…it's an anus!" Ananus says.

"Ooooh! A sign from Heaven!" Tad squeals.

"Nay, quite the opposite," you reply.

A loud rumbling builds up from deep within the monstrous ass.

THHHPPT!!! A deafening farty explosion rips through the sky as the nastiest diarrhea the world has ever seen starts spewing out like a geyser into the air, raining down on everything and everyone in sight.

"Woe is us!" a priest cries, covered head-to-toe in the foul-smelling mess.

Of course, you and your crew remain miraculously spotless and dry, but everyone else is left slipping and splatting around in the disgusting muck.

"Enough!" Ananus cries. "Have mercy on us, Jesus!"

"Who is this man?" a priest whimpers. "He who can summon the bowels of Hell straight from…the bowels of Hell?"

"Mayhap the Son of God. Mayhap the Son of Lucifer," another offers.

"You're damn skippy," you reply.

You clap your hands and the diarrhea fountain dries up with a cute little squeaky poot. The massive hiney retreats back into the earth. You proudly face the priests.

"Did that completely flip your lids, or what?" you say.

"Leave this place," Ananus snivels. "You win this time, Jesus, but we'll be back. And it'll take more than a gusher of doodoo to stop us."

"Any time, any place," you reply, turning to your disciples. "I don't know about you boys, but I could use some fresh air. These Pharisee assholes smell like a mountain of old donkey turds."

Speaking of mountains, you see a cool-looking mountain in the distance and you feel the urge for a good hike right about now…

Turn to PAGE 65

14

Even though you don't fully understand how a baptismal figures into the grand scheme of Creation, you reckon that it will do you little good to be baptized by an un-baptized person.

Plus, you made up your mind when you first laid eyes on John that you're not going to let this scraggly weirdo dunk *you* before you can dunk *him* first, especially with all of these witnesses around.

Planting yourself firmly in the pebbles under your feet, you lunge for John's mid-section and spear him backwards into the water. His head goes underwater for a split second before he can regain his footing and grab at your neck.

The crowd goes nuts.

Thrown off balance and forced to lean back in a painful position, your knees buckle and you go under for a moment. John throws all of his weight on top of you, holding you under.

Beneath the water's murky surface, you hear what sounds like a warbly, muffled chorus of boos and hissings.

You realize that the crowd is behind you all the way.

The crowd's support seems to give you energy and you break John's hold and burst out of the water.

Sweeping John's legs with one foot and pulling his hair with your hands, you push John beneath the surface for a second time, sending the crowd into another cheering frenzy.

Thinking you've bested your opponent and won the match, you release John and turn to leave, but he takes this opportunity to jump onto your back and bite your ear.

Deftly slipping one hand under his leg and grabbing his throat with the other, you hoist John the Baptist above your head and hurl him into deeper water.

A vicious body slam!

You hear several "oohs" and "ahhs" from the crowd as you swim over to him. You mug to the crowd as you strain to hold his head under the water.

When his limbs stop flailing and his body goes limp, you push away from your defeated adversary and climb back up on the shore, where your adoring fans await.

Simon Peter Timothy beams and holds up a large wad of money. He must have suckered some people into placing bets on who would baptize whom.

Apparently, you were the underdog.

A chubby little man runs up to you, his hand extended.

"That was some great baptizing out there, kid," he says. "You almost killed that John the Baptist fella! You ever think of breaking into the world of professional baptizing? With the right manager, you could really go places."

This is honestly one career path you had never considered, but it sure sounds like fun.

"Hey pal, why don't you make like a buzzard and buzz off," Simon Peter Timothy tells him sourly. "We've got bigger fish to fry."

You're too exhausted from all the baptizing to disagree with Simon Peter Timothy, so the guy waddles off, disappointed.

Simon Peter Timothy turns to you.

"Speaking of fish," he says gleefully. "Let's go hit up the beach in Galilee! We have enough cash to rent a chariot and eat a fancy meal on the way! Then we can get caught in the fishermen's nets and pretend that we're dolphins."

Even though you did that twice last week, it somehow seems like a terrific idea right now.

Turn to PAGE 17

Those pissant pansy-ass panty-waists, you think. *I'll give them something to really freak out about.*

You hoist yourself over the side of the boat and step out into the choppy waters. However, instead of splashing into the water and sinking like you normally would, you walk right along the top of it!

The waves are a little tricky to navigate around, but pretty soon you've got the hang of it. It might be kind of fun to stand on top of a wave and ride it all the way to shore. But that's an experiment for another day.

You stroll a few yards away from the violently tossing boat.

"Hey, guys! Look at me," you yell above the storm.

The disciples stop panicking and watch you dance a little jig on top of the waves.

"Be not afraid, you silly seamen!"

Simon Peter jumps up on the ship's railing and calls out, "Can I come out there with you, Jesus? That looks fun!"

"Sure! All you have to do is believe in me and—"

SPLOOSH!

Before you can finish your sentence, a huge whale pops out of the murky depths, swallows you whole, and disappears back beneath the waves.

"Well, never mind that whole Messiah deal," says Simon Peter. Everyone on the boat is more frightened and confused than ever.

Meanwhile, you're busy being pushed through the smelly innards of a sperm whale.

You remember hearing folktales about a man named Jonah who lived for forty days in the belly of a beast like this before being spit back out onto the shores of Nineveh.

You, however, only last about three minutes.

THE END

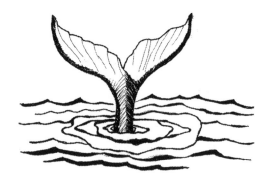

You reach the shores of Galilee with no trouble and are greeted by the wonderful sights and smells of the fishing boats returning home with their nets full of rotten, dying fish.

You and Simon Peter Timothy splash out into the surf, toward some men wrestling with one of the nets.

"Hullo!" Simon Peter Timothy calls out. "Got any jellyfish you don't want?"

"Narrr, we gave the jellyfish to the leperrrs to eat," one of the men says with a frown. He is completely hairless and wears an eye patch, giving him the appearance of a gigantic pirate baby.

The other man looks queerly at you. "Hey, is your dad a carpenter out in Nazareth?"

"Yes, his name's Joseph Christ and I'm his son, Jesus," you answer.

"I thought so. Your father sold us the wood that we used to make our boat. It started falling to pieces within a week," the man says bitterly.

Embarrassed, you don't know how to respond.

The man sticks his hand out to you, scales and fish guts smeared all over it.

"Well, I'm Simon, but you can call me Simon Peter, and this is my brother, Andrew, but his nickname is Timothy," he says.

You shake his hand and turn to your friend. "Simon Peter Timothy, meet Simon, who is called Simon Peter, and his brother Andrew, who is sometimes called Timothy. Andrew Timothy and Simon Peter, meet Simon Peter Timothy, whom I like to call Andrew on certain occasions."

Suddenly, you hear a cry from one of the nearby fishing crews and you see a net full of weird-looking fish spill its contents into the sea.

Within seconds, the water around Simon Peter Timothy's legs bubbles up and turns red. He begins thrashing about wildly and screaming in anguish.

"AAAUUUGGGH!!!!"

"Damn! The piranhas ate their way through the net again!" Simon Peter yells. "Let's get out of here!"

You rush toward the shore, and looking back, you make the gruesome discovery that your childhood friend Simon Peter Timothy has been reduced to small chunks of flesh and bone floating in the surf.

Boy, now you've really screwed up. At this moment, you know that you won't be going back home for quite a long time, if ever.

Turn to the NEXT PAGE

18

"Arrr, what a waste of a good net," Andrew growls over your shoulder. "This happens every single time we go piranha fishing!"

"Rest in pieces," Simon Peter says, surveying the carnage.

"Sorry about your chum," Andrew says. "Errr, I mean your buddy, who just got turned into chum."

"Gee, thanks," you answer weakly.

"Well…that was our last fishing net," Simon Peter says. "What're we supposed to do now?"

The two men look at you expectantly.

"I dunno. I'm bummed and don't feel like doing much of anything," you say. "Maybe now would be a good time to do some aimless traveling, thinking about life, et cetera, et cetera."

"Sounds like fun! Can we come along?" the two men say in unison, simultaneously dropping their fishing gear and cutting their boat free from the shore.

"Uh, sure," you say, feeling a mild uneasiness in your stomach, which could be from all the dead fish at your feet or because you just lost your best friend in the entire world.

The three of you start slowly walking along the edge of the water.

Turn to PAGE 30

"Now Judas, I'm sure you are a nice man and a loyal, selfless Messianic follower, but I've gone over the numbers in my head, and at this point, it just doesn't make any sense for me to add you to my crew," you say. "I'm sorry."

You shake your head and give Judas a big thumbs down sign.

He scowls at you, confused and angry.

"Aw, why not, Jesus?" Philip pouts.

"Because, counting all of you guys and myself, that makes twelve and if we had Judas, it would be thirteen and thirteen is an unlucky number," you reply. "Plus, don't we already have a Judas? That guy's name is Judas, right?"

"Nope! It's Simon," Simon, the guy who you thought was named Judas answers.

"Well isn't that something?" you say, scratching your chin. "Anyway, we're heading off to some place in Judea now so don't bother following us, Judas."

You turn and start to walk away.

"You haven't seen the last of me, Jesus!" Judas screams.

Before the other men can react, he is behind you with a sharp dagger, slitting your throat.

You bleed out in seconds.

"There's a new leader in town, boys! This is my gang, now," Judas yells, dropping your limp body and spitting on it. "Forget about that little queef-puff Jesus Christ. I'm Judas Christ and I intend to show these damn Jews who the real king of them is!"

At first, your followers are frightened, but they are easily impressed and resigned to follow any man who proves that he's tougher, smarter, and more righteous than their previous leader.

Judas takes over your ministry, and thousands of years from now, churches will echo with songs such as, "Judas Loves Me, This I Know," "O, What a Friend in Judas," and "Go Tell It On the Judas" – all because you had to be such a snob…

THE END

You tell your friend to go on and have fun without you. Nothing to do now but head into the wilderness with only the clothes on your back and Perchy's dried-up little poopoos on your shoulder.

Unfortunately, you've never seen a map of this rough wilderness (mostly because no one has ever survived in it long enough to make one) and you soon find that you are one very lost man.

You wander around for days and days, eating nothing and drinking only the sweat and tears and saliva that you can squeeze out of your own body. When you run out of sweat, you get upset and start crying, and when you run out of tears, you remember your sweat and you start salivating, and when your mouth dries up, you get worried and start to really sweat.

It's a pretty cool cycle that keeps you alive for a while longer, but it's also disgusting.

After what seems like weeks, you're deliriously rolling about in anguish on a mountaintop when you hear a strange voice calling your name.

"Jesus...Jesus..."

"Who's there? Mommy, is that you, Mommy?" you hoarsely whisper back.

"No, silly. It's me, Satan," the voice replies. You turn to see a bright red man that looks like what you think Satan would look like.

"Yes, it is I, Beelzebub, The Lord of Darkness, the Devil, Lucifer," he says, bowing. "Or Lucy, for short. I'll even answer to good old 'Lu,' if you don't like dealing with all those extra syllables."

You must be losing your mind. You're talking to Satan, the supreme evil source of the world's suffering? Is this really happening?

"What do you want with me?" you whisper. "I'm just a regular guy."

"Uh huh...right. You know, I'll be honest with you, just this once, even though you're not being honest with me," Satan says. When I heard God was sending His own son down to Earth to piss all over my parade, I kinda expected to see someone, you know, more impressive and powerful. Less puny and pathetic."

You weakly lift your middle finger up at him.

"Boy, you are one hot mess of a Messiah right now, aren't you?" Satan says, his voice filled with mock pity. "I don't know what you'll do first—starve to death or die of thirst. But you won't do either if you listen to me. Let's make a deal, Christy-poo..."

Turn to PAGE 135

22

About five minutes after you've buried yourself under a pile of eucalyptus leaves, you spy Judas and his group burst into the clearing and wake up your disciples.

A couple of soldiers smack them around a bit and demand to know where you are. Not surprisingly, Philip cracks right away and tells the soldiers that you went to pray at yonder Prayer Rock.

From your hiding spot, you watch a few soldiers tromp over to yonder Prayer Rock.

"There's nobody here but some stupid turtle!" one of the soldiers calls out, holding up the turtle that you were talking to a few minutes ago, the same turtle that happens to be inhabited by the spirit of the Almighty God, creator of the universe.

Your eyes go wide and your heart feels like it might thump right out of your chest at any second.

"Well, fuck! If he's not there, then he's either gotten eaten by wolves or he's fallen into a sinkhole," Judas calls back. "We better search the rest of this garden and torture the other disciples before we jump to those conclusions, though."

"All right," the soldier answers. "What should we do with this turtle in the meantime?"

Judas throws his hands up in the air. "Huh? Kill it for all I care! What kind of stupid question is that?"

"I don't like the way this little fuckface is looking at me," the soldier calls back.

Now you're not sure if this is how it works or not, but you have a hunch that if he kills that turtle, he kills God. And if he kills God, the rest of reality might not be able to hold itself together for very long.

With mounting dread, you watch the soldier lift his sword high into the air.

You let out a blood-curdling scream and jump up from your pile of leaves, but he's already ramming the blade deep through the turtle's shell, completely skewering your Heavenly Father to death.

Your brain barely has time to register the explosion of sound and light that follows as the universe fails.

Everything goes purple.

THE END

"Verily, verily, I say unto you," you begin.

You tell a long, rambling parable about a man who cuts off his own foot to make his neighbor's wife jealous. Halfway through, you forget where you were going with it and you trail off, hoping nobody notices.

A quiet moment passes. Even your disciples look confused.

"Excuse me, Mr. Jesus," a young boy says. "Why do you always speak in those silly parables?"

"That's a fantastic question, my child," you respond. "The answer to that lies in the parable of the snake that slept through the harvest. Verily, verily, behold a young snake who did sleep through the harvest…"

You improvise another story, gesticulating wildly and including lots of obscure slang words that you've heard teenagers using. As parables go, you think it's pretty exciting, but before you can finish, another man interrupts you.

"This parable is terrible!"

"Oh really, sir? Well aren't you quite the little poet and didn't even know it?" you reply, grinning and looking around to see if anyone is laughing with you.

Nobody is.

You start telling the classic story of how you turned the water into wine.

"Enough! We've all heard that one and it's not even a parable," a woman screams.

"Yeah, let's throw this bozo off that cliff over there," a man yells. Others shout in agreement and a mob moves towards you.

You backpedal toward the cliff's edge.

"Ha! You've really done it this time, Jesus," Thomas sneers at you. "We're dead meat."

"But I just fed these people five thousand warm, tasty meals," you exclaim. "And from thin air, no less! How quickly they forget…"

"Perhaps we should offer them some of our silver," whimpers Simon Peter.

"No!" snaps Judas. "I need that silver! I mean *we* need that silver. Oh the precious silver…"

"Some of these men look like they're ready to rip our clothes off and ravage us on the spot," Thaddeus says, a hint of curiosity in his voice.

Once again, this situation might call for some creative divine intervention.

Turn to the NEXT PAGE

You hold up your hands to the advancing crowd.

"All right, all right. Let's everybody just chill the eff out for a minute," you say.

Suddenly, all of the angry people freeze in their tracks. You look at your disciples, wide-eyed.

"Jesus...you've turned them into statues," whispers Simon Peter. "And they're ice cold to the touch."

"I've never seen anything like it," John mutters.

"Yarrrrr," adds Andrew.

"Mmmm. Frozen mansicles," Thaddeus says, giving one guy's cheek a tentative lick. "Yummy."

You gently push a little girl and she falls over, breaking into a million jagged pieces. You look down at your hands in awe.

"I am so fucking cool," you wonder aloud. "I mean...uh...for their sake I hope this is only a temporary condition...and just in case it is, let's get the hell out of here before they start to thaw!"

Before you lies a forked road. To the left is Jericho. To the right is Bethany.

You aren't sure what fate lies in store for you at either city, but it's another hot day in Palestine so you better hurry up and make your blind, arbitrary decision already!

If you head to Bethany, turn to PAGE 54

If you go to Jericho, turn to PAGE 142

A few days and a dozen sermons later, you're on the outskirts of yet another village that is abuzz with your arrival. You pass by some ragged tents and a powerful stench hits your nose.

"Whew! Must be downwind of a leper colony," muses James #1.

"Whoa! Lookout!" screams James #2, pointing at a gang of men wrapped head to toe in filthy rags shuffling toward you.

"Ack! Horp! Hellllpppp usssssss, Jeeeeesusssss," one of the pathetic creatures moans.

The lepers start gesturing wildly and jerking their limbs around. Toes and fingers fall off here and there.

"Eww eww eww," Thaddeus says. "Leper people are such icky yuck-yucks!"

"They must want you to heal them using your amazingly wonderful touch, my Jesus," says John.

"Ha! As if he could even heal leprosy," sneers Thomas. "That's the worst disease in the entire world!"

"Hmmm…Thomas's absolute doubt in my abilities is certainly justified here. Leprosy is one disease I've never tried to cure," you say warily. "And what if I can't cure it? Will I catch it? And if so, can I later cure myself of it?"

"Ha! Probably not," Thomas replies.

"Blorg! Herf! Kombutcha!" screams one of the lepers.

There is something heartbreaking about these wretched lepers twitching about in front of you, all hopeless and literally falling to pieces.

Even though you've never healed leprosy, you have tackled similar things, like the time a wolf chewed off your ox's leg and you made a wooden leg for it, allowing it to serve as a beast of burden for another three years instead of being slaughtered and eaten. Well, that wasn't much of a miracle, more darn good carpentry and a knack for animal husbandry.

But back to the question at hand: Should you risk contracting leprosy or just let them all die?

"Jeeeeeeesuuuuuuuth," hisses one of the lepers whose upper lip appears to have rotted off. "Hey. Hi, Jeesuuuth. Hiiiiii!"

Tad was right. Eww.

If you pretend that you didn't hear the lepers, turn to the NEXT PAGE

If you heal the lepers, turn to PAGE 114

Somehow, even though you are the irrefutable Son of God with infinite compassion and mercy, you can still be a heartless bastard at times.

And this is one of those times because you just can't muster up the courage to lay hands on these filthy creeps.

You start whistling and continue on your way, avoiding eye contact with the lepers. One of them rips off his own ear and hits you in the back of the head with it, but you pretend you didn't feel anything and keep walking to the next town.

Word of your blatant miracle snobbery spreads through the leper colony like, well, leprosy and soon enough, scores of angry lepers start infecting the clean population of the nearest village. Leprosy is everywhere!

Before long, Palestine is one huge, ever-expanding leper colony.

It's so overwhelming, in fact, that you don't even get requests to heal other diseases anymore. The half-rotted masses flock to you, and although you heal every case as fast as humanly possible, it's always too little, too late.

The leprosy mutates and spreads, eventually building up an immunity to your healing powers. Within a few months, every human being (including yourself) and most armadillos on Earth have been stricken with the disease and everything is pretty funky all-around.

Mankind's doomed. Way to go.

THE END

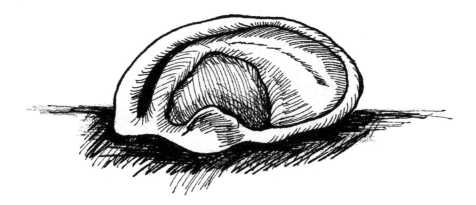

You are led a few miles away to a large clearing filled with a crowd of moaning, malnourished people. Everyone appears to be in great distress, some curled up sunken-eyed and lifeless on the ground, others clawing at their protruding rib cages.

You send James #1 around to assess the situation and he returns a few minutes later with grim news.

"We've got four thousand men here. Not sure how many women and children since they're not as important as the men. But there's a lot of them, too, and they're all starving to death."

"Gee. That sounds like a real shameful thing to see," James #2 says, munching handfuls of corn out of the swollen cornsack he's carrying around.

"Starvation? How can such a barbaric thing happen in these advanced modern times?" you wonder aloud.

"Apparently, they heard you were coming to a nearby village," James #1 replies. "So they all traveled here and have been fasting for weeks."

"Fasting?" you say, shocked. "Who told them to do that? And why for such an ungodly long amount of time?"

Out of the corner of your eye, you spy Bartholomew sneaking away from the scene.

"Stop right there, Bartholomew," you boom, halting him in his tracks. "What did you do? Confess everything to me right now."

"Jesus…honeypot…" Bart says with a devilish grin. "Yes, OK, I did tell these people to fast, but I thought we'd have ourselves a nice, hungry crowd here and I had a sweet deal lined up with all these food vendors who were supposed to meet us with ox patties, ass stew, bird cakes—the whole she-bang. We were gonna make a killing! Anyway, none of them showed. Something about some busted donkeys, a dust storm—"

"Clam it up, Bart," you interrupt. "It's damage control time. Have we got any food?"

Everyone digs around in their robes (or in Matthew's case, his beard), turning up with nothing more than a few morsels and crumbs. Mysteriously enough, the Jameses' cornsacks are nowhere to be found.

"Yar! All we've got arrrr seven loaves of bread and fourrr little fish," Andrew reports grimly.

Turn to the NEXT PAGE

28

"No! Those fish are my pets! And they're not for eating," says Philip.

"You can have your pets back after we're done eating them," Simon Peter tells him.

"Oh goodie!" Philip shrieks.

Philip's such a moron, you think. *All somebody has to do is pull a little wool over his eyes and he shuts right up.*

Hmmmm...fooling people and shutting them up...

You can't really feed this many people in such a short amount of time. But you've just thought up an idea for a quick fix.

It's kind of stupid.

Well, it's really stupid, but it might buy you some time. If it works, though, it'll be your largest miracle to date.

Or you could teach the people some simple agricultural techniques (which honestly they should already know by now) and they can grow their own food. They've already got all this empty land lying around...

If you "feed" the hungry multitude, turn to PAGE 6

If you teach them how to grow their own food, turn to PAGE 156

The next morning, you apologize to your disciples.

"Sorry I lost my temper yesterday, guys," you say. "I promise it won't happen again. Not only was I pissed off at those people defiling the temple, but I felt like if I didn't do something drastic, the world might one day be overrun by megastores that mask their shady business practices with greatly discounted prices for their inferior, cheaply-made products. Thanks for helping me prevent that from happening."

They assure you that it was no big deal and you all head back into town to check on the temple.

Along the way, you stop at a fig tree for a quick breakfast. But alas, the tree is barren.

"Stupid fig tree," you scream. "You better make some figs for me right now or you'll never sprout another fig ever again!"

"Arrr, you be yelling at a tree tharrr, Jesus," Andrew says.

You glare at him. "Shut up, you hairless freak! I want some motherfucking figs inside my goddamn mouth right this minute!"

"Maybe it's not fig season," James #1 timidly suggests.

No figs are forthcoming from the tree. You wave your hand, and the fig tree withers into the ground.

Bartholomew looks at his withered hand wistfully. "Man, JC, you really stuck it to that fig tree," he says nervously. "Shriveled it right up."

"Guess you're still in a funk, huh, big guy?" John offers, patting your back.

Mischief shines in Judas's eyes. "Yeah, Jesus, you feel like starting some trouble? Maybe opening a few jars of whoop-ass on some Pharisees?"

James #2 jumps in. "Heyyyy! You know what we could do instead? We could redirect all of this angst and negativity into love. I know this leper named Simon here in town and I'm sure he'd like to cook you up a nice, calming breakfast. What do you say to that?"

"Booooring!" Judas replies. "Let's go into town and torture some priestly-types. They've certainly been torturing you long enough."

"Love. Peace. Understanding," James #1 says, stroking your hair. "Turn the other cheek, big fella."

If you fuck with the Pharisees, turn to PAGE 44

If you chill out and eat at Simon the leper's house, turn to PAGE 60

30

A few days later, eleven men are following you instead of just two. Taking Simon Peter's advice and walking along the beach was a bad idea.

Something strange is happening. People, particularly depressed and lonely fishermen, are drawn to you like locusts to a wheat harvest. You fear that the local fish-based economy of Galilee might really start to suffer soon.

You turn and face the small crowd of expectant faces.

There's Simon Peter, the first guy you met, along with his completely bald, one-eyed pirate brother, Andrew—both of whom still dress (and smell) like dirty fishermen. Although you've asked them to leave all of their possessions behind, they still carry harpoons and chum buckets, just in case they come across a good fishing spot.

Next are James #1 and James #2—a pair of twins who are extremely overweight, a rare condition in this rugged day and age. They claim that it's a gland thing, but if that were true, you would've healed them of their fat by now. Lord knows you tried. James #1 wears a robe with vertical stripes, and James #2 wears horizontal stripes. That's literally the only difference between these two lazy, relatively useless, fat men.

John, also a pudgy little fellow (but in a cute way), is a nerd, but he's your favorite new friend, thus far. There's something about those chubby little cheeks of his that you just can't pinch enough. He can be a total kiss-ass at times and he tends to write a lot of poetry about you, but it's only because he adores you with all of his heart, which is what you'd like every human being to do, so he doesn't bother you too much.

Then there's Philip—undoubtedly the stupidest man you've ever met. Inside his skull, you won't find one instinct, the slightest hint of an original thought, or one ounce of any kind of learned knowledge. You find it hard to believe that he's survived this far in life without losing any limbs, walking off a cliff, or drowning in a bowl of water.

Bartholomew…either he's your most important follower or he's an extremely talented bullshit artist. He's smart, but he's also a bit of a creep, and when he gets all pushy with his ideas, he really gets on your nerves. Sometimes he makes you wonder if he's following you or leading you.

Thomas. You really liked him at first, but lately he's been a real Negative Nancy. Cursed with the unlovable face of a psychopath and prone to inexplicable bouts of violence, you suspect that Thomas might one day commit a murder, and you hope you're not around for it. But having a guy like him around for random scuffles will be nice.

And Matthew, what can you say about Matthew? He's got the largest, bushiest beard in Palestine and he uses it to store all kinds of things, including a family of squirrels and enough drinking water to last you and your crew for weeks. He's also a depressive writer-type, so you try not to engage him in conversation too often.

Then there's Thaddeus, sweet Thaddeus. For the first few days that he followed you, you honestly believed he was an incredibly unattractive woman. But now you know that he's just an extremely effeminate, gay, homosexual, gay man who loves men.

Supposedly, there's another guy named Simon following you around, but he's got such a nondescript face and personality, you can't quite remember what he looks like. If you recognize him in the future, you should tell him to get lost unless he can prove himself vital to your mission, whatever the hell your mission might be.

As you scan their eager faces, you sigh, not looking forward to disappointing all these desperate weirdos who look up to you like you're some sort of saint…

Turn to the NEXT PAGE

"Listen up, guys," you say. "Simon Peter, Andrew, James, John, Philip, Bartholomew, Thomas, Matthew, James #2, Thaddeus, and uh, am I forgetting anyone?"

"Me, Simon!" Simon calls out from somewhere in the small crowd of men.

"Ok...you," you stammer. "Look, we need to talk—"

Bartholomew cuts you off, "Come on, JC! I told you to call me Bart!"

You scowl at him for interrupting you and suddenly his left hand withers a little bit.

You are both shocked. Did you just make that happen using your mind?

"I'm sorry, Bart. I don't know how or why your hand just shriveled up," you say, annoyed. "We'll fix it later. But what I'm trying to say is that I don't get why you people want to follow me around."

"Because you're the glorious and handsome Son of God and you're going to preach throughout the entire world that the kingdom of God is at hand," John shouts.

The others harrumph in agreement.

"Really? You think the kingdom of God is nigh upon us and that I'm His kid?" you say. "Huh. That's cute. John the Baptist told me the same thing the other day."

You're the Messiah! That might explain why you've been having all those weird spiritual dreams lately.

"And don't forget, the Messiah can perform signs and wonders," one of the Jameses cries.

"And miracles!" the other James adds.

"Miracles, eh?" you wonder, looking at your hands. "So that's why I've been able to defy the laws of physics and cure diseases with nothing but the sheer power of my will for the past few weeks."

"The laws of what?" Matthew asks.

"Never mind," you quickly reply. "Let's table the I-am-the-Messiah discussion for a while, guys. It gives me the heebie-jeebies."

Just then, a dark, thickly-bearded man walks over to your group and Philip excitedly pats him on the back.

"Hey, Jesus," Philip says. "Can my friend Judas come hang out and follow you around like the rest of us? Pretty please? He's the coolest!"

Turn to the NEXT PAGE

34

"Gee, I don't know, you guys," you reply. "I was about to say that eleven dudes are just about all I can handle right now. My life is getting all crazy and I can't afford another mouth to feed. I can't even afford my own mouth, to be honest."

"Oh, lighten up, Jesus," Thomas says.

"Yeah," Thaddeus adds. "You know you never can have enough men in your life. At least, that's what I say to myself all the time when I'm thinking about men, which is quite often."

"I agree. I think twelve is a nice round number," Bartholomew chimes in. "You know, Philip says that Judas here even thought up a nifty name for our group - 'The Disciples.' How does that sound? It's way better than my dumb idea - 'The Christians.'"

You pause, deep in thought.

'Disciples' does have a nice ring to it. You still prefer the name you came up with, though – 'The Jesusians,' although nobody else seems to respond to it, no matter how often you've tried to organically work it into conversations for the past week.

What to do about this Judas fellow? He seems like a nice enough dude, but there's something you just don't trust about him. He never seems to look you in the eye.

Perhaps he's just got a lazy eye, though. And perhaps you could fix that for him with your new awesome Heaven-sent powers…

If you tell Judas to scram, turn to PAGE 19

If you allow Judas to become your twelfth disciple, turn to PAGE 137

Days later, you're lying around and hanging out with your crew on a ship heading to the town of Caesara Philippi.

During a lull in conversation, you casually mention your recurring dream in which you return to Jerusalem and then somehow redeem the souls of every human being in the history of the world through your excessive physical suffering. You tell them how you think the dreams are God's way of telling you to do this.

Your disciples sit stunned for a moment, visibly upset at this news.

"You sure the dreams weren't about some other Jesus?" John asks.

"Yeah, I'm sure it was me," you reply.

John weeps.

"Relax, guys, I don't think anything bad will happen to me," you say. "It's no big deal. I mean, yeah, I'll get betrayed into the hands of my enemies and they'll probably put me on trial, slap my wrists a little. Maybe I'll do some jail time, eat some yucky prison food. But in my dream, I was hanging out with you guys again in three days. Then we all go spread my message of love and healing to the rest of the world. Actually, I'm not totally sure about that last part. It's still a little fuzzy."

"So who's going to betray you?" Judas curiously asks.

"Oh, I imagine the high priests and Pharisees and Sadducees and all those religious jackasses," you say.

"Hmmm...I bet they'd pay a pretty penny to do that, too," Judas mutters, then off your quizzical look adds, "Uh, I mean, I bet I'd make *them* pay a pretty price if they did something terrible like that to you, Jesus. Those fuckers."

"Oh! I almost forgot," you snap. "Simon Peter, you were in my dreams, too. I got betrayed in a garden at night and you denied me three times before the next morning's cock crowed."

"Excuse me. Whose cock does what to who?" Thaddeus asks.

"Me deny you? No way! Three times, you say? That's stupid. Turn my back on my Messiah? Shut up," he says. "I've never denied anything three times in my entire life!"

"Yup," you nod firmly. "Oh yeah, and I just remembered that all of this shit is supposed to go down within, like, the next few days or so."

With this revelation, the disciples burst into a round of incredulous babbling.

Turn to the NEXT PAGE

36

"Cool it, guys! This is obviously an important thing for me to do as humanity's savior," you say. "I need to start saving people. Instead of having to sacrifice animals all the time to make God happy, I'm going to be the sacrificial animal for everyone now. It's like a one-time thing and poof! All your sins are forgiven and you get to spend Eternity in Heaven. Plus, it's not like they're going to actually put me to death for being such a badass Messiah. I do too many good things for people."

"So what if a guy commits a *really* bad sin?" Judas asks. "Like, oh, I don't know, he sells his Messiah out to his political enemies. You're telling me that once you perform your magical hoop-te-doo, in a few days, it won't matter, because all he has to do is ask for your forgiveness and then that traitorous bastard can still go to Heaven when he dies?"

"You got it," you smile. "Look at Judas over here being so smart."

"Fuckin' 'ey. I love this plan," he smirks. "Mark me down as one of the saved, please."

"Hold on one slippery second," Thaddeus says. "Under the current holy laws, we have to sacrifice stuff to be forgiven for our iniquities. The reason I don't do forbidden things, like make out with cute men all the time, is because it's a pain in the ass—a bad pain in the ass, mind you—to go buy a calf, or raise one from scratch, and then slaughter it, and drag it all the way to the temple. So if you save us and wash away all of our sins or whatever, I can diddle men all day long and then just beg for your forgiveness?"

"Yeah, I think that's one way to put it," you say, scratching your head.

"Oh, I get it now. You're simply taking away our accountability as responsible adults," Tad squeaks. "Thanks, JC!"

"Yarrr, the whole thing sounds fishy to me," Andrew says. "Bad fishy, mind you. I don't think you should do it, Jesus."

Others grumble in agreement.

"Honestly, guys, I appreciate your concerns for my well-being, but my selfless redemption of humanity is not really open for debate at this point in time," you say, exasperated. "I just wanted to keep you all in the loop. The ball is already rolling downhill beyond the point of no return, ok? I'm your savior and you're either with me or you're against me."

Matthew raises his hand. "Let me play Devil's advocate here. Why go through with this whole betrayal thing to save our souls? Why not just redeem everyone right now? Like, just say the magic words and make it so, if you have that power."

You sit there dumbly, unable to think of an answer to that.

"Yeah, and by the way, why has God been wasting our time for thousands of years with all the dumb traditions we have to do?" Bartholomew asks.

"Yeah, I easily spend half my disposable income and a bulk of my workday doing stupid temple sacrifices and prayers," Matthew adds.

"Now *that* I do not know," you admit. "God doesn't tell me everything. Or anything, really. I just do whatever He vaguely instructs me to do in my nightly visions. But I do know this – we have to keep blindly trusting Him. Or else."

"Why drastically modify our religious system like this?" Simon Peter asks. "If it ain't broke, why fix it? Sure, it sucks to slaughter animals and waste tons of food on altars all the time, but it's worked for our ancestors, all of whom I assume are happily chilling up before the throne of God in Heaven right now."

"No, I—" you start, then stop and think. "Um, well, that's…wait. I need to save everyone because…uh…the Devil! Yeah. The Devil is Satan and he's, like, the opposite of God and he lives in Hell and if you don't love me and listen to all I have to say, you have to go live with Satan in Hell when you die. Get it?"

"Huh?" says Philip.

"Yeah, what he said," says Thomas.

You fold your arms and silently look at your disciples.

"You know what, Jesus? You've changed," James #2 says bitterly. "Something's different about you. And not something good, like a fun new haircut. Something bad, like chronic halitosis and gum disease."

"It's like you're not the same Jesus I left my three wives, ten children, and a successful tannery in Galilee for," James #1 says.

"Yeah. It's because shit's starting to get real, son," you say, staring daggers into his eyes.

You spend the rest of the boat ride arguing, but don't seem to get anywhere. Everything sure seemed a lot simpler when you first started out on this journey.

Hopefully, this isn't a sign of things to come for your new religious movement…

Turn to PAGE 85

38

"Hold onto your shepherding hood, Tommy boy," you say, licking your fingertip and sticking it in the wine jug.

You pull your finger back out and taste it. Hmm…it's either water drawn from a well that someone dumped a dead pig in or it's really good, potent red wine!

You pass the jug around and everyone who tastes it goes crazy for it.

A local wine connoisseur even cheerfully declares it "a light, crisp little vintage with shades of juniper and minor refreshing echoes of pepperberries."

You bless the other jugs and everyone starts pouring drinks and handing them around to one another. Most of your disciples gladly partake in the wine, and since you're such a sucker for peer pressure, every time a jug passes by, you take a hearty tug out of it.

Somber drabness quickly dissolves into generic, drunken merriment. Even the bride comes out, grabs a jug, and retreats with it back into the honeymoon hut.

At one point, the groom runs over to you and shakes your hand.

"Thank God you showed up here, Jesus," he gushes.

"You mean thank me," you slur. "Or thank God. We're the same people. Person. Even though He's my dad. Um…the Holy Trinity or whatever."

"Well, your obvious daddy/identity issues aside, I really can't thank you enough for saving my wedding today," he says.

You give him a sloppy wink.

"Oh I'll save more than that if you give me some time."

Bartholomew slinks over and slips an arm around your shoulders.

"Jesus, darling, baby, let's hit the road. The local winos are starting to sniff around with cups of rainwater for you to bless. And I also don't like how those angry local vineyard owners over there are looking at you."

You drunkenly counter with, "You guys…fish for little fishies, but I'm gonna teach you…how to fish for men if you follow me…or lemme follow you…uh, something something. And ye shall be the salt o' the earth…or the light, sugar-free gelatin powder of the world, if you're watching your weight."

"Yeah, Jesus, keep it up! That's the good stuff," says Matthew, scribbling madly at your elbow.

"What whiny, long-winded garbage are you writing now, Matthew?" Thomas bellows at him.

"I'm calling it 'The New Testament,'" he answers. "Or maybe 'Stuff Jesus Said.'"

"Gee, that sounds like a real page-turner," Thomas sarcastically sniffs.

"Oh, leave him be, Thomas," James #1 says. "Besides, it's not like 2,000 years from now people will be reading his silly papyrus leaves and believing it and dedicating their lives to its teachings."

"Wow! You really think that's a possibility?" Matthew asks, rolling up his scroll and storing it in his massive beard. "Sheesh, that's a lot of pressure for me to live up to."

"You guys knock it off. Our number one priority right now is to get the big guy sobered up and back on the preaching circuit," Bartholomew says.

You let loose a loud hiccup and have to swallow back a mouthful of alcoholic vomit.

"Yarrr. Heave ho," Andrew says while roughly hoisting you up over his shoulder.

You barely remember kissing your mother and sister goodbye before your disciples carry your drunk, stumbling ass out of town.

Turn to PAGE 157

"Uh, are you certain that the scriptures specifically mention picking *corn* on the Sabbath?" you ask.

"I think so," one of the priests replies.

"Was it corn on the cob, creamed corn, popped corn, or corn bread?"

The priests look at each other fearfully. "Um, the scriptures don't specifically specify which form of corn—"

You cut him off.

"Uh huh. I thought so. I ask you all to turn in your Bibles to First Hezekiah, chapter twelve, verse eighteen. And verily I say unto thee," you say unto them. "The Lord God did create fifteen different ways to consume corn and all of them are good. And woe unto he who says that you should not eat corn at any time. Also, woe to any raven who does eat of the corn."

The priests stand in shocked silence.

Looks like you've somehow out-scriptured the priests! Way to go!

After a short, frenzied conference amongst themselves, the priests dispatch a small mob of people to catch the raven and stone it for disobeying the scriptures.

After the raven's distressed squawking dies down, the priests scurry off, leaving you and your group to finish eating in peace.

"Great thinking with that corn business back there, Jesus," John say, corn spraying out of his mouth with every word. "You used it to get us out of a problem, then into one, then back out of another problem!"

"Yes, I think that it was a perfect testament to corn's phenomenal versatility," you reply while rubbing corn all over your face to exfoliate your skin.

"And spouting out all those old, obscure scriptures. Why don't you ever remix that stuff into your sermons?" Matthew asks.

"Oh I made that all up," you say. "The old scriptures are so boring. 'This guy begat that guy and so-and-so begat whoever the fuck, yadda yadda.' Blech! I like to come up with my own material on the fly, improvising and playing off the audience's energy. You know, like those standup comedian guys do down at the arenas right before they get torn to pieces by wolves and tigers."

"Hey, Jesus, look at me!" Philip screams.

You all turn to see Philip attempting to squeeze an entire corncob into his ear. Blood trickles out of the side of his head and he smiles dumbly at the sky.

Just then, you hear a groan and turn to see a pallid man weakly crawling toward you.

In your signature kind and gentle Son of God fashion, you rush over and embrace him.

"It looks like this dear man is dying of thirst," you exclaim, cradling his head to your breast. "Bring him some sun-dried corn kernels, and quick, goddammit!"

Thaddeus hurries over with a raw corncob and starts roughly shoving it in and out of the exhausted man's gaping mouth at a rapid pace.

"That seems to have helped. Thank you, Tad," you say. "Looks like he has something to tell us now, so you can stop with the corn."

"Oh, just a little longer, please. This is fun," Tad replies, relishing in the in-and-out rhythm of the corncob.

Thaddeus yelps when you slap the corncob out of his hand.

The man looks up at you graciously and coughs up a few golden kernels.

"They…they're all…starving, Jesus," the man hoarsely whispers. "Please…you gotta… help…them."

"Say no more," you tell the man, clamping your hand tightly over his mouth. "Lead the way to these suffering people, and once again I will shove my tallywhacker in the face of evil, all the while teaching you indispensable lessons concerning faith, love, and humility."

"But wouldn't you like to know what we're going up against?" John meekly asks at your elbow.

"Nope!" you retort. "I just want to dive balls-deep into this one, balls-to-the-wall, pedal-to-the-metal, balls and all, once and for all, 'til death do us part, see ya, wouldn't wanna be ya."

Before anyone can respond, you heave the dying man up into your arms and rush off in the general direction that you think he might have pointed.

Turn to PAGE 27

42

Galilee is a madhouse. Every decrepit, sickly person for miles around is here, pleading and moaning for your touch.

Over the next few days, you perform all sorts of miracles you never expected to do:

You climb up on a roof and heal a severely palsied man who was hanging out on a roof for no reason.

You meet a man with a clubbed foot and you make his other foot clubbed so he has a matching pair.

A woman complains that she's been having a heavy flow period for a year, and with a snap of your fingers, you grant her early menopause.

Diarrhea, gangrene, lupus, hemorrhoids, shingles – your healing touch can banish them all. Even death itself is no match for you.

Some guy leads you to his house and shows you his daughter lying dead on a table, but you immediately lift her to her feet and announce that she was just in a deep sleep for the past week!

Face it, Jesus. You're the shit.

In the span of a week, you've become acquainted with every part, function, condition, abnormality, and fluid of the human body. You wonder if these poor fools ever bother visiting doctors.

By far, the worst people to deal with are the village hypochondriacs – you touch them, make them whole, and they come back days (sometimes even hours later) with some new imaginary affliction for you to heal, some ridiculous new demon to cast out.

To break up the monotony of the hands-on Messianic blessing and healing routine, you have to start getting creative with your techniques.

One day, a blind man approaches you, asking to have his sight restored. You can heal blindness without even touching him, but you want to give all the onlookers a story to tell their grandkids.

With a sideways glance at the skeptics, you spit into the dirt, pee on the spit, poop on your pee, then you scoop it all up, and rub the mucky goop right into the man's sightless eyes.

To the crowd's amazement, the man's eyes pop open.

"I can see!" he cries. "Hey, why'd you just smear gross-ass dirty fucking mud and shit in my face?"

You smirk and nod your head in a certain way that signals to your disciples to muscle him away before he makes a scene.

Another man grabs your arm and excitedly mouths something to you. You can't understand what he's saying.

"Heal my brother, Jesus," a nearby woman says. "For he is dumb."

Another easy one. But you'll give it a little flair.

You stick your fingers in the man's mouth, pull on his tongue, and stretch it out a few feet until it's nice and taut. You let go and it ricochets back into the man's mouth with a squishy thud that knocks him off his feet.

"Hey everybody! I talk now," he jumps up and screams. "Blueberry poopoo wing-wang macdonald farts!"

"Oh no. He wasn't just silent dumb, he must be dumb in the head, too," the woman sadly says. "Can you heal that, Jesus?"

"Sorry, I can't fix stupidity," you reply. "I found that out a few villages back. Stupid is forever."

"Then you may as well take away his tongue again," she dryly replies. "I don't want to listen to this nonsense for the rest of my life."

You look at the babbling idiot and grant her wish, silencing him once again.

"Wow. This is some crowd turnout, Jesus, especially for a Sabbath," John says.

Holy crap! You forgot it was the Sabbath, which explains why that pack of high priests has been giving you the stink-eye all day. According to the Holy Law, you're not supposed to be doing anything, even healing people, on the Sabbath.

Whoops.

"Look out! Make way!" someone yells.

The crowd parts like the Red Sea, and a twisted, drooling, shivering mess of a human being is placed on the ground before you.

"Ugh. What's wrong with that?" asks Thaddeus.

"And *what* is that exactly?" adds Simon Peter.

"A maimed, deaf, mute, blind, possessed, lame leper," a man answers. "And she's got a pretty bad case of dandruff, too. Can you fix her up, Jesus? She's my wife."

You've already done a lot of healing today and you're tired. Plus, it is the Sabbath and you know if you don't stop now, the infirmed masses will just keep coming. But this wretched soul on the ground looks like she can't wait until tomorrow. Should you continue to heal or should you rest?

If you keep healing, turn to PAGE 11

If you rest and talk to your disciples, turn to PAGE 107

44

"I've got a cheek you can turn," you tell James #1, cracking your knuckles. "My left ass cheek. And then you can kiss it! Those Pharisees ain't seen nuthin' yet from this Messiah! I'm gonna solve every last problem I can find in this whole damn city."

You push the crazy oil-dumping lady out of the way and lead your party out into the street, ready to make some serious lemonade from all the lemons that have been piling up in your life.

An hour later, you are up to your sternum in healings, exorcisms, signs, wonders, and various undocumented miracles.

Since you first busted up into the temple in the center of town, you've been fixing every major and minor crisis you can find—every crooked tooth, scraped knee, bruised forearm, bad haircut—you name it.

If it's wrong, you're making it right today.

Understandably, the scribes and Pharisees are livid about this, and they have no problem voicing their concerns to you.

"Woe unto all you hypocrites," you haughtily say, curing a child's botched circumcision.

"Whoa indeed," one high priest says to Ananus. "He's crossing some serious lines here, healing people's pee-pee's like that."

"Cross, you say?" Ananus replies. "Hmm…crosses. That gives me an idea. Follow me, fellow cretins."

Ananus and several of the Pharisees grab Judas and sneak off behind a small curtained-off area of the temple.

You look up from the retarded duck whose wings you were straightening and wonder aloud, "I wonder what's going on with Judas over there behind that curtain?"

Thirty or so silver coins drop and tinkle out from behind the curtain.

The priests and Judas curse and scramble around in the crowded space, trying to pick them all up.

John taps you on the shoulder and says, "Pardon me, Jesus, but I've got some good news and some bad news."

"Give me the bad news first," you say.

"Ok…we've completely run out of ailments to heal in this town. That's also the good news. Hallelujah!"

"Well, in that case, glory be to God, but also, goddammit to Hell," you mutter.

All out of human diseases and now you've run out of stray dogs, house pets, and other domesticated beasts to heal!

What's next? Heavenly crop irrigation? Insignificant carpentry miracles? Divine vermin extermination?

Just then, you hear some muted cheering coming from somewhere on the other side of the temple and Judas walks out from behind the curtain, looking even more shifty-eyed than usual and getting big pats on the back from all the Pharisees.

For a moment, you think you catch a glimpse of Satan in the crowd congratulating Judas, too.

What dirty business does that rat bastard have here today?

Eh, maybe you're just delirious and seeing things that aren't there because you still haven't eaten anything all day. You're even starting to feel a little weak from it. Damn fig tree!

You've obviously riled up the Pharisees, so your mission is definitely accomplished for the day.

Perhaps you should call it quits and grab a bite to eat. You have a funny feeling that something intangibly significant happened today and it might be your last earthly meal for a while, perhaps even for Eternity.

Better make it something yummy...

If you eat your Last Supper at a fancy restaurant, turn to PAGE 56

If you eat your Last Supper at someplace quick and cheap, turn to PAGE 88

46

"Let's make a deal. You baptize me first and I promise that I'll do you some other time," you say. "Cross my heart, hope to die, stick a needle in my eye."

"I hate to say it, but that's not good for me, Jesus. I could be arrested, imprisoned, and executed any day now," John the Baptist replies. "You know how it is for us prophets lately. The religious leaders get nervous when other people come along and start hogging the spotlight. It's getting harder and harder for zealots like me to keep our heads on our shoulders."

"All right," you answer. "How about you give me your biggest, sloppiest bappy right now, then I come back tomorrow, get a second bap, just to be sure I'm good and bapped-up, and then I return the favor and baptize you? That cool?"

"Fair enough," John replies a bit cautiously. "But if you back out on your promise, I'm going to hunt you down, peel your skin off your bones, and wear it all around town every Tuesday."

You make a mental note to actually keep your promise to this maniac, then you hold your nose and allow John to dunk you underwater for a second.

You break the water's surface, gasping for air (you have tiny lungs). Not surprisingly, you don't really feel all that different, you know, baptized or whatever.

As you trudge back up to the riverbank with John, the crowd politely cheers for you.

Just then, a dove floats down from the heavens and alights upon your soggy shoulder.

"Lo and behold! This dove is the Holy Spirit of the Lord coming down to bless the one true Messiah," John shouts. "I present to you all, the savior of humanity, the Son of Almighty God, Jesus Christ!"

People start applauding and weeping at this announcement.

"Um, actually, this isn't the Holy Spirit. It's just my pet dove, Perchy," you explain. "He's just hungry. See?"

You scoop some manna off the ground and hold it up to Perchy. The bird pecks at the manna and coos with delight.

John looks dejectedly at the crowd.

"Aw shucks. I thought you were the Chosen One," he murmurs.

"Hmmm…if so, nobody told me," you reply, confused.

John's face turns crimson with rage. "And to think that I almost let *you* baptize *me* in front of all these nice people! Hither thee gone from this place, thou knave!"

He hurls a rock at you and it strikes Perchy, who screeches and flutters off into the clouds.

That's no way to treat a bird. This guy's got some nerve!

"Jeez, you don't have to lose your head over this, dude," Simon Peter Timothy says, grabbing your arm and pulling you away from the river.

John the Baptist shakes his fist menacingly at you as you leave the scene.

"Come on, Jesus, we don't deserve to be treated this way by some wacko religious nut," Simon Peter Timothy says reassuringly. "Let's head to Galilee and see if the fishermen caught any sharks today."

You agree with Simon Peter Timothy, and even though you love watching the fishermen mercilessly club sharks to death, John the Baptist's strange words keep echoing in your head.

Are you really the Chosen One, the Messiah, the dude that all the scriptures have been predicting for centuries?

Ever since your miraculous virgin birth, which was supposedly foreseen by ancient prophets and celebrated by those shepherd guys and three wise men, you've always felt like you might be sort of special.

Simon Peter Timothy happily chatters on, but you're finding it hard to focus on what he's saying.

It might be nice to have some time alone to think about this whole Son of God business.

There's a wilderness nearby where you could do just that.

If you go to Galilee with your friend, turn to PAGE 17

If you head into the wilderness alone, turn to PAGE 21

48

"This is Poppa's house—a holy temple, not a market-mart," you grumble seconds before you turn into a one-man wrecking ball—knocking over the money-changing tables, licking or taking bites out of all the fruits on sale, and overturning the cobra baskets.

Merchants and illegal loan sharks flee in terror.

In the midst of your destructive rage, you stumble across a row of small wooden cages filled with sacrificial birds.

You see a sign that reads, "Bulk pigeons—Buy 1, Get the Rest for Free!" Inside a cage underneath that sign, a familiar-looking dove flaps excitedly in your direction.

"Perchy!?! What are you doing here on sale at below wholesale prices?" you cry.

"Please forgive me, Jesus!" a shop-owner pleads. "I did not know it was your bird! I will increase its asking price, if you'd like, so that others may perceive it as a more valuable pigeon!"

You deliver a stunning roundhouse kick into the shop-owner's chest. He flies back, demolishing several cages and sending birds fluttering about everywhere.

"Perchy's a dove, not a pigeon, you dumb son of a bitch!" you scream, spittle flying into the man's terrified face.

You grab a nearby bullwhip and start literally whipping everyone and everything in sight, unleashing all of your pent-up confusion, anger, and insecurities.

It's both impressive and sad.

By now, your disciples have gotten in on the action and are quickly clearing the remaining merchants and consumers from the temple.

You grab the last cowering money-lender by his lambskin lapels and grumble, "Listen up, scum. I'm gonna walk outta here, head back to Bethany, and lodge there. Yeah, you heard me. I'm gonna lodge like the fuck. Then tomorrow, when I'm done with all that lodging, I'm gonna come back here and there better be a helluva lot of worshipping going on or I start tearing the whole place apart, brick-by-two-ton-brick."

"Yes, Mr. Jesus!"

He scampers off, coins scattering on the ground behind him.

"Let's blow this den of thieves," you tell your disciples as you survey the temple's wreckage.

And you do just that.

Turn to PAGE 29

"O ye of little faith and penises," you snort.

With an impressive display of upper-body strength and grace, you shimmy up the boat's mast, clutching onto the top with your thighs and spreading your arms out as if to embrace the thunderous clouds.

"I command thee, all manners of rain and wind and general storminess to immediately piss off!" you shout.

Instantly, the sun is shining, the waters are calm, and the wind becomes a gentle breeze tinted with the scent of lilac and buttercups.

"Whoa. I didn't say the sun had to come out," you snap at the sky. "You can still be nighttime."

The sun quickly drops and a lovely, full moon springs up in its place.

"That's better," you say, and then slide down the mast to the deck, dusting off your hands like what you just did was no big deal.

Your disciples are speechless.

"What manner of man is this?" Simon Peter whispers to Thaddeus. "Pass it on."

"When man loves a man, it's bliss," Thaddeus whispers to John. "Pass it on."

"Which manta can grant me a wish?" John whispers to Philip. "Pass it on."

As your disciples feverishly whisper back and forth to each other, you wring out your clothes and head back to your waterlogged bed, ready for whatever challenges lie ahead.

Turn to PAGE 159

"This'll learn ya not to deny me thrice, Simon Peter," you mutter.

Tapping into energy reserves that you didn't know you had, you spring up from the ground and shift the cross onto his shoulder.

Simon Peter's eyes go wide as he realizes what you're doing.

"Here ya go, Jesus," you say, addressing the stunned Simon Peter. "Allow me, a simple man named Simon Peter, to finish carrying your cross for you!"

You grab the cross back from Simon Peter. The guards start kicking him, and you hobble down the street, dragging the cross the rest of the way to the crucifixion plaza in Calvary.

Lucky for you, the guards can't tell that they're now carrying the wrong man because their helmets offer such a limited range of vision. As for the crowd, they're too bloodthirsty to notice your switcheroo, either. They just want to see some good old-fashioned hangin' and dyin' today!

You drop the cross in its designated area (a big, cross-shaped outline drawn in chalk on the ground) and the guards thank you for your help.

You quickly dissolve back into the crowd and watch Simon Peter suffer a pointless crucifixion for the sins of all humanity. It looks like an unbearably painful and uncomfortable experience and you're thankful that you're not in his sandals right now.

This quirky turn of events leaves you free to figure out a quiet, less violent, and self-destructive way to redeem mankind from their iniquities in the near future.

Pretty sly, old man. Pretty sly, you think.

Just then, a woman grabs your arm.

"Oy! Here he is, guards!" she screams. "This guy's one of Christ's disciples. I confronted him about it earlier and he tried to deny me!"

A guard seizes you and grumbles, "Yeah, he looks like one of the disciples. Not even worth wasting a good cross on. Let's throw him to the dogs!"

Moments later, they toss you into a pit filled with ravenous mongrels that tear you to pieces. The head of Rome's Department of Torture and Capital Punishment keeps these dogs on the edge of starvation in case of execution overflow situations such as this in which they need to quickly dispose of a dishonest, cowardly piece of garbage like you.

THE END

52

You reach over and cast the demon out of the unclean child. It's a surprisingly mild and unspectacular experience. The demon jumps into a loaf of bread and impales itself on a knife. Satan curses you and disappears in a poof of smoke, just like he *always* does.

"Big whoop," you say. "Kid's clean. Yawn. Onto the big city!"

"Thanks for healing my child, Jesus," the kid's father says. "Might we hear one of your nice sermons now?"

You think for a moment, then reply, "Eh, I'm not really in much of a preachy mood. Matthew, give this man some papyrus pamphlets and let's be on our way. Don't forget what I said about leaving that fire and water lying around. Real safety hazards for the kids."

Later, right before you tromp through the city gates of Jerusalem, Bartholomew grabs your arm and stops you.

"JC, you gotta make your triumphant entrance into Jerusalem in style. This isn't one of those hick villages we've been bouncing around in for the past few months. It's the big leagues. The people will want to see a suave, sophisticated, and most importantly, scripturally-sound Messiah."

Judas grabs your other arm and continues, "An old prophecy says that the King of Kings will ride into Jerusalem 'sitting upon an ass and a colt, the foal of an ass,' whatever that is."

You ask your disciples where you're supposed to find an ass and a foal of a colt thingy in such a short amount of time. They shrug.

"I know a guy who knows a guy who's got a camel," Matthew suggests. "It's a little rundown, but it should be good enough."

This is silly. It seems like one of the lesser-known, unimportant prophecies. You've already fulfilled most of the big ones anyway.

Of course you want to live up to the ancient prophet's expectations, but the average believer probably doesn't care about their Messiah's ground transportation, just that he shows up and makes everything all right.

Maybe you should walk. It's simple, humble, and it's gotten you this far, hasn't it? But you've never ridden a camel. That might be fun...

If you ride an ass and colt, turn to PAGE 68

If you walk, turn to PAGE 147

If you ride a camel, turn to PAGE 155

"To hell with your silly cheek-turning, James. I'm taking this voluptuous young woman to be my bride," you calmly announce. No one makes a sound as you scoop her in your arms and carry her out the door.

The two of you hide out in an abandoned hut for the rest of the day, whispering your life stories and ambitions to each other. Her name is Mary (named after her mother and every other woman in the world), and like all other women, she has lived an insanely tedious and suppressed life. But you're going to save her from that, aren't you?

Later in the night, you steal a donkey and you travel together for a few weeks—honeymooning, experimenting with mind-expanding herbs, and redefining your views on religion and creativity.

After a while, you track down your disciples, most of whom have been busying themselves with side projects—tagging along with other prophets, working on some of their own solo sermons, or simply partying with groupies and keeping their old apostolic glory days alive.

You convince them that you're ready to work again and that you want Mary to be part of your group. She starts co-writing your sermons, and much to the other disciples chagrin, preaching the sermons herself as you stand idly by. When she lays her own hands on some infirmed people, Simon Peter tells you that he and the boys don't consider Mary as one of the Apostles and that you're not the same Messiah since she appeared.

You dismiss his criticisms like you have for the past few months, though. Eventually, the frustration is too great, and after several legal suits and counter-suits as to who owns what of your past and future ministry materials, you and the Apostles split up for good.

It doesn't bum you out too much, though, for you still have your precious Mary. The two of you return to Galilee, move into a luxurious hovel, and continue to collaborate on miracles, prophecies, and sermons.

Critics argue that the work you're now producing is inferior to what you once did, but fuck those wankers, man. You're more popular than any other man (or musical group) who has ever lived. Your religion, Christianity, will never vanish or shrink. Your disciples were thick and ordinary. You're right and you will be proved right.

Years later, while taking a daytime stroll near your apartment, a crazed fan whom you had given an autograph to earlier in the day, jumps out of a doorway and fatally stabs you. Thousands of your fans turn out for your funeral, celebrating your life and mourning not only the loss of the man you were, but also the loss of what you could have been.

Imagine all the people you could have saved…

THE END

54

Immediately upon your arrival to Bethany, you encounter a group of women weeping outside of a tomb. Two of them turn and approach you.

"Thank Heavens! You must be that Jesus guy and his twelve apostles," one of the ladies sniffs.

"How did you know?" asks John.

"He looks like a Jesus and he's got twelve scraggly men following him around like all good apostles are known to do," the other woman says bluntly.

"Huh. I always thought I looked more like a Terry," you say. "But yeah, I'm your Jesus. What's up?"

"Glory be to you. I'm Mary and this is my sister Martha," the woman says, shaking your hand.

You hug them both and remark to Martha how strange it is to meet a woman not named Mary.

"I know! I'm an utter freak!" she cries. "But aside from that, would you mind if we dump all of our problems on you for a moment, Jesus?"

"Will it matter if I say that I do mind?" you reply.

Completely ignoring your answer, she throws herself at your feet and cries, "It's terrible, Jesus! Just dreadful! Our poor brother Lazarus died and has been dead for over four weeks!"

"We've all been out here weeping and gnashing our teeth for a month," Mary adds. "It's getting rather tiresome and it's not doing any good, to be honest. Think you could help us out with a little resurrective action?"

James #2 pulls you aside and whispers, "This guy died weeks ago. You've never rezzed anyone who's been dead for that long. What if it doesn't work?"

"And you just know that guy's gonna stink like week-old pig shit," whispers James #1 in your other ear. "Do you really want to have to smell something gross like that?"

"He's probably deader than any other dead guy I've ever seen," Philip murmurs.

You worriedly glance back at the boo-hooing Mary and Martha. The poor things just want their brother back.

"By the way, Jesus, you should also know that Lazarus supported Mary, myself, his wife, and eight kids," Martha says. "No pressure or anything."

Mary stomps on her foot.

"Don't listen to her, Jesus. We'll be fine," Mary says meekly. "We won't starve or anything. There's plenty of dirt for us and our many malnourished children to eat."

"Sheesh," you say under your breath. "No pressure indeed."

In your endlessly benevolent heart, you know that you can't just walk away from this debacle. But can you truly resurrect Lazarus?

It sure couldn't hurt to try.

But then again, if you do resurrect him, all the other weepers in this town are going to get their lady undergarments in a bunch and start begging for you to resurrect their dads and husbands and long-dead kids.

This could get real messy, real fast.

In hopes of keeping everything simple, perhaps it would be best to solve this problem with an old fashioned optical illusion...

If you really resurrect Lazarus from the dead, turn to PAGE 84

If you pretend to resurrect Lazarus from the dead, turn to PAGE 132

56

You inform your disciples that you'd like to grab a bite to eat at someplace nice, especially since you could be betrayed at any moment. This creates a huge argument amongst the twelve because of course each one has his own opinions about where you all should dine.

You instantly regret telling them that this might be your Last Supper. Now it's got too much significance attached to it.

By the time they finally settle on a place, Le Desert Rose, it's pretty late in the evening.

"The goat tartar at this place is *to die for*," Tad gushes as you walk over to the restaurant.

"I'm so hungry, I'd pretty much die for anything at this point," you reply. "And I guess I will be soon anyway…"

Luckily, the restaurant agrees to seat your large party as the last table of the night. But as soon as you sit down and look at the menu, you realize that it's way too pricey. Judas says he's got plenty of silver and can easily afford it, but everybody else is broke, as always.

You kindly inform the manager that you happen to be one-third of the Holy Trinity and that you will soon exchange your mortal life for his eternal one, but he's still not willing to give you any kind of a deal, especially because you came in with such a freaking huge party.

Twelve disciples! Why'd you have to be so greedy? Three disciples just wasn't enough for you, was it? Ugh!

You spend the next half hour feigning interest in the menu while ordering the free bread roll baskets and water (with lemon), but eventually the waitstaff sees through your ruse and they kick you out.

By now, it's too late to get a table anywhere else and all the shops are closed, so your only option is to return to camp and stare at a fire until you fall asleep, which is what you've done almost every night of your miserable life. You think about how everybody loves to sit around and watch fires and how mankind will probably never invent anything more interesting to sit and watch at night than a good fire.

The next morning, you awaken to the smell of Thaddeus' hand-rolled cinnamon rolls. As you're positively famished, you heartily gobble them up.

Too heartily, in fact, for in the middle of swallowing your fourth cinnamon roll, a pebble that was accidentally baked into the sticky, sweet dough gets caught in your esophagus and you start choking.

If only there was some universally-known method for dislodging food from people's throats before they choke to death on their food…

THE END

58

"If you can't beat 'em, join 'em," you say and immediately plop down a deposit for a nice little corner lot of shop space in the temple.

"Technically, Jesus, you did beat 'em yesterday," Matthew says, consulting his scroll of notes. "I'm just saying..."

But you don't hear him, though, because you're in full-blown business mode now.

You send out half of your disciples to scour the town's marketplace for antiques and any other old thing that looks like it could be cleaned up and resold.

You order the other guys to roll out your shop's rug, flattening it smooth and straightening it every which way to maximize the amount of foot traffic and commodity space.

Within the hour, Tad presents you with an armload of fine wares – crusty animal pelts, multipurpose stones and sticks, and even some great mud!

Who knew Tad was so naturally talented at antiquing?

You carefully and tastefully arrange the antiquated items on your shop rug and paint a sign that reads: "J's Knick-Knacks n' Things."

Your resale shop is an instant hit. People shuffle on and off your rug faster than Matthew can ring the little bell you gave him to ring so you know when people enter and leave your store.

By the end of the first day, you're divvying up a nice stack of shekels and denarii for everyone in your group.

But splitting everything thirteen ways means you're going to need many more high sales days like today, however, if you're going to turn a decent profit by the end of this fiscal year.

Surprisingly, business is just as brisk over the next few weeks. You even have to expand onto a second rug to keep up with the demand. This allows you to pull in twice the money!

One day, you're approached by a private investor who says that he likes what he sees and he offers you a proposition to install franchises of "J's Knick-Knacks n' Things" in temples, mosques, and altars all over the country.

After discussing all the financial particulars, you come to an agreement and sign a bunch of legal papyrus-work that cements your status as a shrewd and successful businessman.

Life is great, and as you lay in your bunk bed that night inside the crowded, yet well-built house that you and your apostles rent out together, you feel confident that you've made all the right choices in life.

The next morning, you enter the temple with your disciples, roll out your store rugs, and open up shop, ready for another great day of commerce.

An hour later, two rough-looking men step onto your rug, and in the blink of an eye, they're all up in your face.

In a gruff voice, one of the men says, "I'm Tenus and he's Booba and this is a stick up!"

Indeed you see that it is, for both of the men carry long, sharpened sticks in their hands and they're aiming them right at your chest.

Your disciples bristle when they see this, but wisely, nobody makes a move.

"No funny business, pal. Just fork over the coins and nobody gets hurt," Booba says.

The friendly color drains from your face and you assume a defiant posture.

"I worked my ass off for several weeks to get this store off the ground and I will lay down my life and die before I let you stomp in here and take that away—"

Before you can finish, the men stab you with their sharp sticks, puncturing several vital organs and making off with all of your cash.

As you lay dying in the middle of your antique-reselling empire, you reflect that apparently you did make one bad choice somewhere along the way in life.

You should've posted a "NO SHARP STICKS" sign at the edge of your rugs.

Sheesh. Did you really believe that you'd get away with running a store in God's holy temple, Jesus?

Shame on you, you money-hungry asshole!

THE END

"Bite me, James #1," you snap. "God wouldn't have given my face cheeks if He didn't want me turning them every chance I get."

You're not crazy about the concept of eating a meal prepared by a leper, but you're starting to feel a low blood sugar headache coming on, so you agree to join Simon the Leper at his house for a late breakfast.

Maybe a full tummy will help clear my mind, you think.

Unfortunately, Simon the Leper's house is as nasty as every other leper's house you've been in and you quickly find that it's not so easy to fill up your tummy while being constantly repulsed.

You bit into half of a dirty fingernail in your buckwheat waffle and you're pretty certain you just witnessed Simon's wife fry up one of her eyeballs when it fell into the pan of eggs.

Oh yeah, James #2 forgot to mention that Simon's entire family also has leprosy.

So even though you've completely lost your appetite, it doesn't seem to bother your apostles much, and you forlornly watch them attack their meals with gusto.

Minutes later, as a peach cobbler dessert (complete with chunks of someone's diseased scalp baked right in) is passed around the table, a woman enters Simon's house, carrying an ornate alabaster box.

Quietly weeping, she strolls over to you and dumps an oily fluid out of the box onto your head.

You sit—depressed, hungry, and blank-faced—as this strange woman smears the odd-smelling goop into your hair.

"Excuse me, miss, but what's in that oil you just douched Jesus' holy head with?" Tad asks.

"It's all pure 100% organic, local ingredients," she answers shyly. "Tar tree oils, skunk musk, and cougar bladder juice."

"Hmph. And I guess you couldn't have given the rest of us any of that expensive ointment," Tad sassily retorts. "What, we're not good enough for your ointment? Why you gotta be wasting it all on Jesus' nappy-ass hair like that?"

"Foolish woman! You could've sold it and donated that money to the poor," Judas says. "Or better yet, donated it to me!"

"You know what I'd like?" Bartholomew says. "Some frankincense with some motherfucking myrrh. Why can't people be bringing us shit like that all the time?"

"Yeah, even just a little myrrh…not necessarily every day, but once in a while would be nice," Matthew whines.

"I don't know what a myrrh is, but I want it now," Philip says in a whiney voice.

You feel the screaming rise up in your chest before it's even pouring out of your mouth.

"Everybody just shut the hell up!"

They all stop chattering and look at you.

"What's happening right now is totally not cool, guys. I don't know who this woman is or why she came in here to dump weird oils all over me. No offense, lady, I'm sure it's a nice gesture and all, but right now I smell like a cedar tree covered in cougar piss, I'm hungry, I've been marked for death by my father, and I miss my home and whatever small, unimportant life I used to live!"

"But Jesus, we—" Simon Peter begins.

"No! Put a sock in it, Petey," you say. "I'm pissed off. And pissed on, apparently."

As Simon Peter ponders exactly what a "sock" is, you glance at the woman who's been inexplicably anointing your head. Even though you're fairly angry at her, you can't help but notice that there's something beautiful and striking about her face.

For a second, a thought dances through your mind that maybe you could take her away from all of this craziness and just get lost in her eyes and soul for a while.

Wouldn't that be fun?

Or you could swallow all of your ungodly anger and work twice as hard at being the best damned savior this world's ever seen, proving your enemies wrong and making your Heavenly Papa proud...

"Don't forget about turning that cheek, Jesus," James #1 meekly suggests over your shoulder.

If you save like you've never saved before, turn to PAGE 44

If you elope with the mysterious woman, turn to PAGE 53

62

"Nobody calls me chicken, Satan!" you say, yanking the laser rifle from his razor-sharp claws and jamming the barrel of it down his throat.

"Hasta la vista, baby," you mutter and then pull the trigger.

Satan's head explodes in a neon shower of goo and demon pieces.

"You did it, Jesus!" Mary Magdelene cries from across the room in her metal cage that's still swinging precariously over the lava pit.

You push some buttons on a nearby control panel and the cage drops her into your arms. Nearby, a door swishes open and all of the orphans rush out towards you, happy to be freed from their prison cells.

"Yeah, looks like I won the battle this time, but I've still got the rest of the war to fight," you say, your muscles rippling beneath your robe and sweat shining as it runs down your perfectly chiseled face.

You push another button on the panel and the monitor shows a video of the real Satan fleeing in a secret submarine. Whatever you just killed was merely one of Satan's demonic goons! He tricked you!

Mary reaches over, kisses you deeply, and places your hand on one of her huge, perfect boobs.

"Forget all of that for now, Jesse," she purrs into your ear. "Let's go home and make the Son of the Son of God."

Right there in front of the orphans, you hike up Mary's skirt and—

HEY! WHAT'RE YOU DOING READING THIS? There's no possible way that you should be on this page. You're cheating!

Were you just flipping through this book all willy-nilly and looking at the pictures until you found one with boobies and firearms in it that piqued your filthy, perverted interests? Do you treat all the Choose-A-Choice Books™ like this? You should be ashamed of yourself!

For being such a terrible cheaty-pants of a reader, your adventure will end here. You don't get to see what happens when Jesus flies back to the good guys' base in his sonar jet and finds out what his next awesome, death-defying mission is. You also won't get to read anymore about Mary Magdelene's fantastic rack and all of the sexy things she can do with her amazingly hot, flexible body.

You know why? Because you're about to get a big fat "THE END" up in your face! And once that happens, you're going to have to put this book down forever because you flipped to this page even though you weren't supposed to and then you prematurely finished the story.

Too bad you had to go and be dishonest like that.

So here it comes, big boy. Hope you're happy. Idiot.

THE END

64

You walk over to the bread and rocks and take a bite, immediately shattering most of your teeth.

YEEOOWCH!!!

It really hurts when you do that.

"Sucker!" Satan screams. "Nobody will have the ability to turn stones into bread for at least another six or seven millennia. That's when genetically modified foods and technology will start getting ri-goddamn-diculous, you know?"

You look down at the bloody stone, its top sprinkled with shards of your teeth.

"No, ah don't. Wha's thecknoloshy?" you ask, your mouth a painful, bleeding mess.

"Guess you'll never know now, will you?" he taunts while jumping around with glee. "Maybe you should wash all that yummy rock down with a piping hot cup of sand, boy genius."

For a brief moment you consider trying to drink some sand, but then you decide it's not worth the effort.

You're done for anyway. You collapse and die with a dry gurgle.

Thousands of years from now, a group of archeologists will be utterly baffled when they dig up your bleached bones sitting next to a few loaves of pumpernickel bread and a glass of lukewarm orange juice.

THE END

Halfway up your ascent of the mountain, your disciples start getting all gripey on you.

"Come on, Jesus," Judas whines. "Why you gotta drag us up and down these mountains with you all the damn time?"

"Yarrr. It be a thousand degrees out here," Andrew pouts. "We be suffering from mild heat exhaustion. Especially the fatties in our group."

"There then," you wave him away. "I just healed all of your heat exhaustion. Quit your bitching."

"We've been running from village to village nonstop," Thaddeus says. "I've worn through five pairs of cute sandals. It's an utter nightmare."

"I thought a hike would be nice," you explain. "To help us relax and clear our minds. Those of us who do indeed have minds to clear."

"But we walk all day, every day," Thomas says. "Why would more walking help us relax?"

"Discipling for you is hard work, Jesus," Matthew says, his beard dripping with sweat. "Let's just find a quaint little village to rest in for a few days."

"My God, I haven't seen this many pussies gathered together in one place since Simon Peter Timothy and I snuck into the women's baths in Corinth!" you scream. "All right, you can all rest here. But I set my mind to climb to the top of this mountain and my holier-than-thou ass is going to climb it."

John perks up. "I'll go with you, JC! Just you and me! Road trip!"

"I'm going too," Simon Peter says. "Too many weird happenings lately. That Satan guy might show up and try to tempt you again. Better take one of the Jameses, too. His tubby girth will help make it look like we're rolling with a big posse."

The four of you split off from the rest of the guys and ascend the hot, stony surface of the mountain, your skin baking and brain sizzling with each step.

By the time you reach the summit, you're all on the brink of succumbing to the infernal heat.

John collapses, begging for water, which, of course, none of you thought to bring.

"Can't you turn water into air?" James #2 pleads with you.

You weakly shake your head no. You're doomed!

Turn to the NEXT PAGE

66

Just then, Simon Peter gathers up some strange-looking mushrooms from under a large boulder and pops them into John's mouth.

"We should all eat some of these," he says, and holds out a few to you. "They store up water in their tissues and I think they're not poisonous."

You chomp down on your mouthful of mushrooms and they squirt a warm, bittersweet juice onto your dry, swollen tongue. As you relish this thirst-quenching feeling, none of you have any idea that you've all just ingested enough psychedelic material to make a full-grown donkey think it can walk on its hind legs for a few days...

Five minutes later, things have gotten weird. You just witnessed John's arms turn into blue serpents and bite his privates off, Simon Peter married himself to a shrub and gave birth to a baby cactus, and you could swear that James #2's head is now running around on James #1's body.

Simon Peter looks up from breast-feeding his cactus child and asks, "Yo Jesus, why you gotta be wearing that white-ass bright as fuck robe like that?"

You look down and indeed your robe is as blindingly white as the sun.

"Yikes! That's some supreme holy shit happening right there," you say, rubbing at your eyes. "I'm all transfigured and what-not."

The mushrooms intensify. Minutes bleed into hours as your group crawls around and completely spaces out.

At one point, Simon Peter stacks up some rocks and branches and calls them his "holy tabernacles for the prophets to sit in."

Seconds later, your mind is blown when the legendary man known as Moses and the world famous prophet Elijah float down from Heaven and land right on top of his tabernacles!

Elijah and Moses float over, pull you to your feet, and the three of you entertain your apostles with a wonderful improvised variety revue filled with duets, medleys, dances, and even a few ribald skits that make Simon Peter blush and repeatedly cover his baby cactus's eyes.

Right when your final musical number ends, a huge white cloud forms above your heads and a loud voice booms out of it, "Great show, son! Moses, Elijah, get your goofy asses back up here to Heaven where you belong!"

"Oh! The voice of the Almighty God! You really are His Son, Jesus," John says, astonished.

God responds, "He's My boy, all right. Better enjoy him while you can because he'll be returning to Heaven soon. Right, Son?"

"Wait, what?" you say, struggling to focus on the conversation. "I'm coming to Heaven? Is that Your smooth way of telling me that I'm destined *to die* for humanity's sins down here? I thought I would just be doing some jail time or community service."

God pauses for a second, deep in thought.

"Um, yeah," God eventually says. "I'm doing this blood covenant kind of thing to absolve mankind of their sins and make it a bit easier for them to get to Heaven when they die."

"Oh," you say disappointedly.

"Somebody's got to spill his blood for that to happen, though. So of course that somebody would be humanity's savior, a.k.a. you. Didn't we already go over this tiny little detail in one of those weird dreams I sent you?"

"No, no, no you didn't, Pops," you answer, extremely bemused. "And let me tell you, now is just the PERFECT time for me to die a senseless death, now that I've finally figured out what I want to do with my life and I'm on a roll with my ministry. Thanks a lot, Dad!"

"Look, I'm the all-knowing, utterly infallible heavenly being here," God angrily retorts. "And I'm sure that I explained all this sacrificial lamb bullshit to you a while back. You've just been too busy living the fast-paced life of a tender, loving Messiah to pay attention to what your Old Man has to say. And that, just like everything else that's wrong with the world, is not My fault."

You stomp your foot and stick out your lower lip.

Not surprisingly, hearing all of this dire news about your earthly mission straight from the Big Guy's mouth has sobered you up quite a bit.

Your head starts to throb.

You flip your middle finger up at the cloud you've been yelling at for the past few minutes. Then you reach over, grab a handful of mushrooms, and chomp your way into another psychedelic stupor.

Fuck it. Life's too short. Let God pick up the pieces.

Turn to PAGE 145

68

You may as well ride the stupid donkey, although you wish God had given the prophets a vision of you riding on a mighty steed or at least something cool and awe-inspiring, like a jewel-encrusted crocodile.

"Go get the foal of an ass colt or whatever the hell it is that I'm supposed to ride," you say.

Minutes later, they saddle you up on a donkey and you ride into the city gates of Jerusalem. Immediately, the townspeople recognize you as the Prophesied One and start laying palm branches down in front of your donkey and chanting things like, "Holy holy holy," "Hosanna in the highest," and "Ride that ass, JC!"

Gee whiz, you think. *This is even sweeter than the scriptures made it out to be! It's good to be the Messiah after all.*

Beaming with pride, you parade yourself through the streets and eventually wind up at the temple. You may as well be a good Son of God and make a quick visit to your Father's house while you're in town. You dismount, autograph a few scrolls and bare shoulders for your adoring fans, and march through the temple doors.

Once inside, instead of hearing a quiet, respectful service being preached, you find a bustling madhouse of activity. Your smile vanishes. They're not just selling holy relics and sacrificial gear, they're hawking decorative pottery, jewelry, sporty tunics, and those awful little bean bag animals that all the children of Judea have been crazy about lately.

Your disciples look at your worriedly.

"There seems to be less worshipping and more shopping going on in here," you say.

"Does that mean we get to go shopping?" Tad asks, which earns him an immediate smack upside the back of his head from Judas.

Looking around at all of the bartering and financial transactions taking place, you think about how this is wrong and blasphemous and a slap in God's face. But you also notice that there are some great bargains to be had and you've got a whole donkey-full of Messiah merch that you could probably unload here for a tidy profit...

If you start kicking people's asses for corrupting this sanctuary, turn to PAGE 48

If you further defile the temple by setting up shop, turn to PAGE 58

You speak the special keyword for demonic transferral between humans and swine.

"Zoinks!"

The demons, having no other choice since you uttered the special word, quickly shuffle out of the man's body and into the pigs. Since they've never possessed pigs before, they instantly freak out and fly off the nearby cliff, squealing to their piggy deaths in the churning ocean below.

The possessed man returns to normal.

"Thank you, Jesus," he says with a warm smile. "Now I can go back to my old life as a fair and honest judge of important criminal disputes. My name is Pontious Pilate and before those gnarly demons possessed me, I was a Governor in Rome. I'll never forget what you did for me today. I promise that if you ever need a favor, no matter how big or small, even if someone's trying to crucify you for heresy or something, I owe you one. Big time."

He trots off in the direction of the nearest city. Everyone cheers and pats you on the back.

But one guy is not cheering or patting - the farmer who owned all those pigs. He approaches you and demands payment for his loss. You explain that you have no money, and offer to pay off the cost of the pigs with miracles.

"Miracles ain't gonna put no food on the table," he says.

You try to tell him that you can probably do that with your powers, too, but he stubbornly refuses and forces you to spend the next few years sifting pig feces out of the mud in his pigpens. It's a terrible, backbreaking job and most days you're so exhausted and dehumanized that you eat right out of the filthy feeding trough with the rest of the pigs.

Years later, when you've finally paid off your debt to the farmer, you are an old, feeble man who can barely walk and no one remembers you or the miracles you once worked.

THE END

70

You smile weakly, "Eh, I can't just stop being God's only begotten son, can I?"

Pilate chuckles. "Yeah, we all kinda turn into our fathers, don't we? Mine was a Roman Prefect, his father was a Roman Prefect, and so on. A long line of drunks and wife-beaters...but I digress. You know, you're all right, Jesus. It's a shame that you're claiming to be the flesh and blood incarnation of the one true God, which is against the holy law."

You nod knowingly.

"You're causing too many problems around these parts," he continues. "And I can't have that, so I have no choice but to sentence you to death. Sorry, but it's my jobby job."

"Oh it's fine, Pilate," you retort. "All part of my plan, actually."

"Really?" he replies, shocked. "And what's the next step?"

"I think I'll chill in the afterlife for a couple days and then come back here, maybe raise myself up from the dead."

"And then..." Pilate seems to be losing his patience.

"Uh, I'll probably say some stuff to all my followers and then I'll go back up to Heaven, continue my ministry in a more hands-off kind of fashion, and just wait for Judgment Day to come around."

"Ok, I don't like you anymore, Jesus," Pilate says, washing his hands of you in a big basin of water. "You know how many guys breeze through my court every day saying exactly what you just did? Earlier today, I executed two other Messiahs, five fanatical prophets, and one guy who's been preaching that the archangel Michael appeared to him as a chicken and revealed to him that the world will end next Wednesday."

You roll your eyes. "Yeah, but *those guys* are all crazy. I'm the real deal."

"That's what they all say," Pilate sighs. "String him up on a big ol' cross, boys. I'd let the people vote on how to execute you, but they always choose crucifixion, the merciless bastards."

A soldier whispers something in Pilate's ear.

"What do you mean we don't have any crosses open? I just had a dozen more constructed last Friday!" he screams.

The soldier whispers again.

"They're not dead *yet*?" Pilate responds. "Man, those crosses make such awesome torture devices. Almost too slow, honestly. Our backlog of crucifixions is getting ridiculous! Ok, let's just release some other criminal and squeeze Jesus right into his slot. How about that psychopathic homicidal child rapist guy named Barabbas?"

The court's audience cheers wildly.

"All righty," Pilate says. "The people have spoken."

An hour after they release Barabbas, he decapitates an innocent toddler. Nobody seems to notice, though, because they're all too excited about your upcoming date with a certain familiar cross-like apparatus.

The next few hours are not very fun for you. The soldiers drag you into the Common Hall, strip you naked, and hundreds of strangers proceed to ridicule your genitalia's size, shape, and coloration.

This is the normal cruel and unusual punishment for a crucifixee. Lord knows you've been a member of the jeering crowd plenty of times, but it really really blows to be on the receiving end of everything.

Once you've had enough, you beg your captors to move along in the crucifixion process. When the soldiers and crowd finally feel satisfied that they've mocked your penis in every possible way, they start dishing out the rest of the standard pre-crucifixion torture activities—tearing out chunks of your beard and pubic hair, smiting you upon the head with a variety of sticks, dangling their spit above your face and sucking it back up at the last second, and ruthlessly ripping the flesh of your back open with a whip made of pottery pieces and bone shards—all the crowd favorites.

Somebody gets the bright idea that since you're the King of the Jews, you should be wearing a crown. But not just any crown. That would be too easy. Instead, you get a crown of sharp, poison-tipped thorns.

Everyone waits while a few soldiers scrounge up some thorns and weave them into a crown-ish shape. It takes them a few tries to get it right.

Meanwhile, you curl up on the ground and try not to bleed to death for a little while longer, although you're not sure why.

They finally finish the crown and wedge it down on your head. The thorns pierce your flesh and scrape along your skull.

Owweee!

A guard informs you that now, per tradition, you have to carry your own twelve-foot, wooden cross down a long, crowded alleyway to Golgotha, where all the real crucifying action happens.

"I don't suppose that you guys could've set up this crucifix thing for me over there already, huh?" you ask a soldier.

"You ever hear of that saying, 'it's my cross to bear?'" he replies.

"No."

"Well this is where it's going to come from." he says with a swift kick to your gut. "So get to bearing it!"

Turn to the NEXT PAGE

72

You begin the long walk to Golgotha. Weakened from all the blood loss and mental anguish, you trip a few times and eventually collapse, unable to carry the mammoth wooden cross any further.

Unbeknownst to you, Simon Peter is three feet away from where you fall, having muscled his way through the crowd in hopes of seeing you one last time.

A lady clutches his arm, "Hey! Ain't you one of them Jesus disciples?"

"No maam," he replies. "It would be foolish for me to show up here if that were true."

That's denial number two, Simon Peter thinks. *Please don't ask me again, lady.*

"You sure?" she replies. "I swear you and Jesus healed my boy's crooked teeth back in Philippi."

Indeed, he sees that her child has a mouth full of perfect teeth.

"My good woman, I sincerely again deny your accusation," he blurts out and then covers his mouth in shock when he hears a cock loudly crowing.

"It's almost noon. Why's that silly cock crowing now?" she asks.

Simon Peter stumbles back in horror and trips, landing on the ground next to you.

"Simon Peter!" you hoarsely say in astonishment.

"Huh? Um, whoever you are, I don't know you, sir," he stammers.

That son of a bitch must've denied you thrice! You knew you heard a cock crowing a few seconds ago!

If you use this opportunity to get revenge on Simon Peter, turn to PAGE 51

If you ask Simon Peter to carry your cross the rest of the way, turn to PAGE 78

You turn to your disciples and whisper for them to follow your lead.

"ROOOOOAAAAR!"

You violently fall to the ground and start thrashing about, tearing your clothes off, and urinating all over yourself.

"Oh no! Jesus has been possessed with demons this whole time!" Simon Peter exclaims. "What a shocking turn of events!"

"Hell yeah! Let's party, bro!" the possessed man shouts.

You gnaw on your fingers and pull clumps of hair out of your head. He stomps on his own foot and bites off half of his own tongue.

Your disciple Thaddeus jumps in front of you and dramatically addresses everyone, obviously loving the theatrics of the situation.

"Christ almighty," Thaddeus adds. "He must have ka-billions of demons up inside of his body! How delightfully dreadful!"

He pretends to faint. Or maybe he's not pretending. You crawl over and hump his leg. A hint of smile creeps across his face.

"Yeah, and everybody knows that there's only enough room for one demon-possessed lunatic in every town," Judas says.

When he hears this, the possessed man stops tearing at his chains and looks at everyone else nodding in agreement with Judas.

"Well if that's how you people really feel," he says, disappointed. "We have no choice but to head out and find a new town to terrify."

The farmers let go of the chains and the possessed man shambles off down the road.

"We had a really swell time here," he mutters and softly waves goodbye.

Once he's well out of sight, the James brothers walk over and pick you up off the ground where you've been foaming at the mouth and faking spasms for the past few minutes.

Everyone surrounds you in a congratulatory manner.

"Yarrr! Way to go, Jesus! He took the bait," says Andrew. "Hook, line, and sinkerrr."

"Hopefully that's the last we'll ever see of him," you say, dusting yourself off. "Hey, Bart, you think we still have time for me to do some serious preaching on top of a mount-like structure?"

"Sure thing, boss. I factored in a few random encounters with demon-possessed psychopaths, so we're actually right on schedule," he replies with a grin.

Turn to PAGE 92

74

The guards take this opportunity to rough you up a bit, tussle your hair, and dress you up in women's clothing. They appear to be having great fun with you. Afterwards, it's time for you to stand trial before Pilate, and they drag you over to his chamber, which of course is on the *complete opposite* side of the monstrous palace!

By the time you arrive there, you're an absolute wreck. A multitude of Pharisees, strangers, and most of your personal sworn enemies fill the room to watch your sentencing.

Pilate calls down from his seat high above you, "So this is the guy who's going around telling people that he's King of the Jews?"

"Yes, your honor," a guard calls out. "He also cut off one of our men's ears when we apprehended him."

The one-eared guard waves his hand in recognition of this statement.

"Jumping Jupiter, I have to stop working these night court shifts," Pilate sighs. "The freaks always come out at night, they say…"

You clear your throat and speak up.

"Actually, I tried to heal his ear—"

"Objection!" Pilate interrupts. "I can plainly see that the man is missing an ear. He probably had possession of said ear before he encountered you, am I right?"

"Well, yes, but—"

"Overruled!" he screams. "Moving along…Is it not false that you do truly consider yourself to be the one true King of the Jews, which we all know is truly false?"

You think about his question for a second.

"Uh, true, I think? I prefer Son of God or plain ol' Messiah, but if you want to call me King of the Jews, I can dig it."

"I thought as much," he responds sadly. "My only option now is to sentence you to an immediate death, and it will probably be the slowest, most painful and cruel death we dastardly Romans have ever invented. We're talking about crucifixion here."

Upon hearing the C-word, the place erupts into cheers and excited murmurings. Surely you won't have to be crucified, right? You would rather have your skin flayed off or get beheaded. You know, something quick, easy, and painless in comparison.

"Order in the court!" Pilate roars. "Let me first say this: I sort of like you, Jesus. You've got a kind face. A nice, soft, bearded, gentle face that I could see printed onto clothing and painted on paintings and replicated in multicolored glass windows in grand worshipping structures."

"Why thank you," you say, blushing.

"So because of that sweet little boy face of yours," Pilate continues. "I'm going to grant you this one brief moment of mercy. If you can give me one good reason not to execute you, then I'll set you free."

The whole room holds its breath in anticipation. This is it. You could get out of this mess right now if you say the right thing.

"Well, Jesus…I'm all ears," Pilate says with a grin.

"Hey, that's not funny," the one-eared guard calls out. "I can still hear you making fun of me, you know."

So, Reason for the Season, what's your reason?

If you don't have a good reason, turn to PAGE 70

If you think you do have a good reason, turn to PAGE 148

If you'd rather give him an immature and stupid answer, turn to the NEXT PAGE

"Fuck you, Pilate," you boldly call out.

He leans forward in his seat.

"Excuse me?"

"You heard it. *Fuck you*. Suck my big, holy weenis."

"Jesus, you just piddled with the wrong Prefect," he replies angrily. "Take him to the Brazen Splitting Drum Wheel!"

The guards drag you outside and into an arena full of shouting people.

In the center of the arena, you see a complicated and terrifying torture device made out of brass, iron, and wood and covered in blades, belts, flames, and spikes.

As the guards strap you onto it, one of them tells you that the Brazen Splitting Drum Wheel is still a work in progress and you'll be the first public execution with it.

Lucky you.

Within minutes, you're being sodomized by a palm tree; hanging horizontally at a downward-sloping angle with a metal collar fastened around your neck that ever-so-slightly strangles you; your limbs are slowly being snapped backwards and pulled up and out of their sockets; and any protruding body parts like your penis, nipples, or ears have been clamped or pierced and are violently being torn from your body.

Later, a heavy metal roller will crush the remainder of your body inch-by-inch while also searing your flesh and peeling it off your bones.

Four days later, when your brains are finally, mercifully squeezed out of your head through your nose and eye sockets, you expire.

The crowd shuffles out of the arena and unanimously agrees that you've just suffered the slowest, bloodiest, most painful execution that anyone's ever had to endure. It's such a horrific event that Pilate has the machine disassembled and burned so it can never be used again.

The good news is that word of your selfless martyrdom spreads all over the world. The bad news is that you violated God's will by not dying on a cross like you were supposed to and He revokes your right to redeem humanity's sinful souls.

Throughout the rest of human history, your billions of misguided believers will adorn their jewelry, clothing, and churches with an extremely vile-looking Brazen Splitting Drum Wheel symbol in remembrance of your suffering today.

But their souls haven't been saved, and neither has yours...

THE END

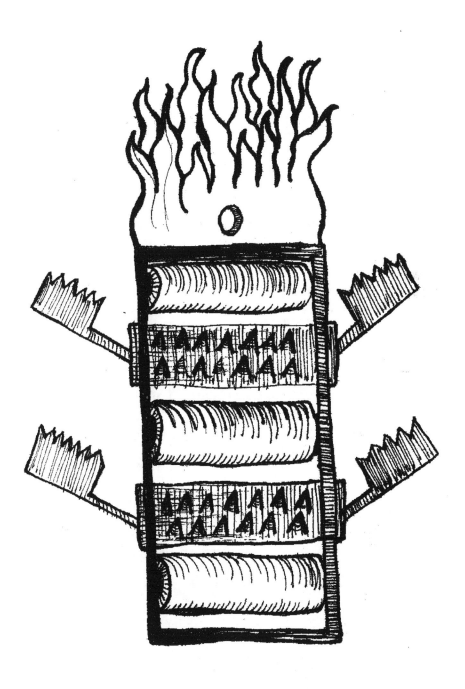

78

That dirty son of a bitch denied you thrice! He should be the one carrying this damned heavy cross all the way to Golgotha, especially if you're the guy who's going through the trouble of dying on it later and then forgiving him for wronging you in the first place!

You give Simon Peter the stinkiest stink eye you can muster at this point, which isn't easy to do since both of your eyes are almost completely swollen shut from all the beatings you've taken today.

"All right...I'll carry it," he hisses at you.

But before he can pick it up, another man slides up under the cross and heaves it onto his own shoulder.

"I'll take it from here, Jesus," the man says with a smile.

"Off the hook! Thanks, Simon!" Simon Peter yelps and runs off.

You watch him go, then turn to this Simon guy quizzically.

"It's me. Simon..." he says. "I was one of your twelve disciples."

"Really?" you ask. "You were one of the twelve? One of the Dirty Dozen? No way. I don't remember you at all."

Just then a nearby cock loudly crows.

"Dammit, Jesus! That's the third time you've denied me!" he cries, dropping the cross and running off.

You look around, hoping for an explanation of what just happened. The soldiers shrug.

One of them pokes you with the tip of his spear and says, "Let's get this show on the road, holy man. Enough of your drama."

"Yeah, save it for the cross, Jesus," another guard says.

"You mean, save *us* on the cross, huh-huh," the other guard adds with a chuckle.

"Ha! Yeah. Our Almighty Savior, this guy over here," another guard chimes in, and everyone shares a nice, big laugh at your expense.

You sigh, stooping to pick up your cross again. You carry it the rest of the way to Golgotha without any further noteworthy incident.

What the fuck, man? No one mentioned that you'd have to carry the fucking thing up a goddamn hill littered with human skulls!

You should've known this would be the case, though, since the word 'Golgotha' translates to "giant hill of death made out of skulls".

You drop the cross in the designated cross-dropping area (there's a sign indicating the spot, of course) and you lay on top of the cross, exhausted.

"Go on," you say to the guards, spreading your limbs out. "Crucify me already. Here, I'll hold the first nail over my wrist for you."

On your cue, the guards set about their crucifying duties—ripping your clothes off (again!), nailing your arms (ouch!) and legs (double ouch!) to the cross, tearing your clothes up (for no good reason!), and hoisting your cross high into the air. The first time they do it, though, you're upside down. Bunch of amateurs, these guys...

Their overseer tells them to pull you down and lift you up the right way. Of course, when they do this, they have you facing *away* from the crowd, so they have to pull you down and put you back up AGAIN.

By now, one of your wrists has come loose from the cross and hangs free (because the newbie guard who nailed it couldn't find a wrist with a ten-inch spike if his life depended on it, which it pretty much does). So one last time, they have to drop your cross back down to the ground, re-nail you, then raise it back into the air.

"Hey, Jesus said he would rise again and I guess he did!" one of the soldiers quips. "Three times already!"

You definitely got the jokester shift of executioners. Before they nailed you up, they dressed you in a diaper and hung a little sign above your head that reads, "Jesus, King of the Jews," with a doodle of a penis and an arrow pointing down at you. The crowd loves it.

"Oh God," you say to the heavens. "Why have you forsaken me?"

"You think you've got it bad?" a voice to your left says.

You look over and see another guy hanging on a cross. On your other side, another guy is also engaged in his own crucifixion.

"My cross is made outta pine and I'm allergic to that shit," the first guy says. "I got a rash on my back that's bigger than my actual back is."

"That's nothing," the other guy moans. "The nails missed all my major blood vessels and I'm barely bleeding. I'll be up here for weeks!"

"Why are you guys up on crosses, too?" you ask.

"I stole a loaf of bread," the guy on your right says. "I'm Tenus."

"And I'm Booba," the guy on your left says. "They caught me stealing goat butter to put on the loaf of bread that Tenus was stealing."

Great, crucified with a couple of thieves, you think. What'll my mother think if she sees this?

You glance down and see your mother in the crowd, shaking her head in disapproval. Aw man! And there's your old date who you never really got to date, Mary Magdalene. Some douchey dude's got his arm around her perfect, virginal shoulders. He's probably felt all over her ankles by now, too. What a terrible time you're having!

Turn to the NEXT PAGE

80

"How about you, stranger? What're you hangin' for?" Booba asks.

"Oh nothing big. Just all of humanity's sins," you answer.

"So, you're one of *those guys*," he says snoodily.

"Ugh," Tenus huffs. "I hope my mom doesn't see me up here getting crucified next to yet another religious wacko."

Looks like you're the meat in an asshole sandwich up here. But before you can respond, one of the soldiers calls up and asks if you'd like something to drink. You graciously accept.

"I wouldn't do that if I were you," Tenus says.

"What do you know? You're just a petty thief," you retort. "You'll probably try to steal my drink from me. I'd like to see you try that."

The guard ties a soaked rag onto the end of a spear and lifts it up to your mouth. You suck on the rag for a second and immediately gag and spit it out. It tastes like they dunked the rag in vinegar. Yuck!

The guards start cracking up and the crowd roars with laughter.

"Toldja so," Tenus says matter-of-factly.

Just then, a strong breeze blows your diaper off and now you're hanging buck naked for the entire world to see.

"Ok, God, you've really forsaken me now," you lament.

You scan the crowd, making eye contact with several familiar faces—your family, friends, and disciples. Most of them look upset, but you can't believe they're just standing around and watching this happen. Even Satan is down there, high-fiving a couple of demon-possessed spastics and making crude gestures at you.

You've got to do something. This is getting ridiculous. You had no idea that your ultimate sacrifice would be so physically and emotionally painful. Maybe it's still not too late to back out of this situation, however.

You haven't lost *that* much blood, and between the two hardened criminals on either side of you, you're sure that you can come up with some kind of caper to get you out of here.

Or you could stick to your word and die like you're supposed to. Maybe God will take some mercy on you and grant you a swift death.

If you hatch a brilliant escape plan with the thieves, turn to PAGE 94

If you meekly continue to die, turn to PAGE 95

82

It's been nearly six years since you took Satan's advice, abandoned your ministry, and left your disciples staring in disbelief as you walked out of that village.

But it's been an interesting six years, and looking back on it all, you can't really complain.

Soon after you set out on your way back home to Nazareth, you stumbled across a bagel shop owner who took an instant liking to you and made you the offer of a lifetime – your very own bagel-making equipment, a small herd of dairy cows, and a cozy little building on the corner of a busy marketplace.

Within a week, you opened up your very own bagel shop - the Cream Cheesus Bagel Depot.

To further separate your bagel shop from those of your competitors, you anointed every customer's order with a little chant: "I bless this in the name of the butter, the bun, and the whole wheat toast."

Since that day, your fate was sealed as a successful pastry baron-to-be and your shop hasn't been able to bake your delicious bagels and assorted savory breads fast enough to keep up with the insane demand for them.

You even jokingly started referring to yourself as "Jesus Christ, the Flav-ior of Humanity."

After your business took off, you acquired four wives, eight kids, and a sizeable (yet lightly-mortgaged) house. You've also put on a few pounds here and there, and your second-favorite wife jokes about all the gray hairs that keep appearing in your beard lately.

Hell, if things keep heading the way they're headed, you might retire soon and run for mayor of this little town.

Life is good. And it's all because on the day that Satan convinced you to start over, you adopted a new motto with which to live every moment of your life by: "No regrets. None."

You even got it tattooed across your shoulders so when your shirt is off, people standing behind you can instantly see what your life's motto is.

And you honestly can't think up a single thing to regret about the past six years.

Here's to the next six being just as awesome. Good job!

THE END

"How do you prefer to be worshipped?" you ask Satan.

"Oh, a generous amount of groveling and moaning and begging for mercy should do nicely," he grins.

You comply, profusely weeping and blubbering at his feet and pleading for just an ounce of mercy, a shred, a smidgeon. Satan laughs like a madman and you stop your sniveling to look up at him.

"You fool," he mutters. "Haven't you ever read the Ten Commandments? You're not supposed to worship anyone but God. He's the one you should be begging for mercy, you nitwit."

"Drats! I knew better than to make a deal with the devil," you say, pounding your fist weakly into the dust.

"The devil? Oh, I'm not really the devil," Satan says. "I'm just some weird-looking guy named Satan who likes to travel the wilderness in search of pathetic individuals who look desperate enough to perform whatever random silly tasks I ask of them."

"That...that's just plain mean," you croak.

"Eh, it helps the time go by," he replies with a smirk.

You clutch at his robe before he trails off down the mountain. In this moment, you know that you are doomed, having wasted your last precious sweat, teardrops, and slobber on Satan's double-crossing feet.

The last sensation you feel is the sharp jolting peck of a buzzard's beak on your dried-up eyeball.

THE END

84

You lovingly place your hands on Mary and Martha's shoulders.

"So you sweet little ladies want me to raise your brother from the dead?" you say. "You got it. Piece of cake."

"What's cake?" Martha asks.

"Oh you're about to see a piece of it, darling," you answer with a cocky smile. "Make mine strawberry."

You stroll over to the mouth of the tomb and call out, "Lazarus, come forth!"

For a moment, everything is perfectly still and quiet. Then you hear a deep, hungry moan rise up from within the dark tomb, followed by the appearance of a gnarly grey hand.

It's Lazarus! Your resurrection worked!

Something about him doesn't look quite right, though...almost ghoulish. He scans the crowd with dead, angry eyes and then lets out a ghastly shriek.

"Good God! He's not alive, he's not dead..." Judas mutters.

"He's...undead," you say, finishing his sentence for him.

Before you have time to stop her from doing so, Mary rushes over to Lazarus with her arms spread wide for a hug.

With lightning quickness, the unholy creature that used to be a man named Lazarus grabs Mary and takes a healthy bite out of her throat. Blood sprays everywhere.

Mary falls to the ground, then picks herself up and turns to face you, the same empty, undead stare shining in her eyes.

The next few minutes are utter chaos—screaming, running, bleeding, more biting. With every bite, Lazarus and Mary transform another human being into one of their zombie brethren.

Somehow, you escape the frenzy with Martha and a few of your fleet-footed disciples.

Months later, you've gotten pretty good at trapping and dispatching of the zombie horde, but every city and village you visit is filled with more and more, and none of the scraggly survivors seem to care much about your miracles or sermons anymore, now that the undead apocalypse has destroyed any hope of living a normal, happy life.

Every day that you survive is a miracle in itself, but you know it's only a matter of time until even those miracles dry up like all the rest of 'em...

THE END

You arrive in Caesara Philippi and immediately encounter…no one? You walk with your disciples down a completely deserted, quiet street.

"What the bejeesus is going on around here?" you ask. "Where are all my desperate, hopeless believers?"

Bartholomew shrugs.

"It be the Sabbath, yar," Andrew says. "And this be a Pharisee town. Therrrr be temples everywherrr."

"Towns like this, they don't even let their cattle work on the Sabbath," Matthew says. "Bunch of tight-wads if you ask me."

"Great!" John says. "We're ministering in a town full of overly-religious Pharisees on their holiest of days right after Jesus just got done telling us that the Pharisees are going to arrest him!?!"

"If Jesus gets arrested here, it's all your fault, Bart," Thomas says.

"Look, I'm sorry, everyone," Bartholomew says. "But somebody needs to invent a better calendar so I can keep my dates straight."

"This smells like a trap. Did one of you assholes already betray Jesus?" Judas asks accusingly. "And if so, how much did they pay you to do it?"

"Calm down, guys. I don't think it's time for my betrayal yet," you reply. "And don't worry, I forgive you, Bart. I'm kind of scripturally obligated to."

Suddenly, all the temple doors burst open and hundreds of Pharisees and priests flood out and surround your party.

Judas was right! You're trapped!

"Ah-ha! We've caught you red-handed, Jesus!" the high priest Ananus sneers.

"You caught me doing what?" you reply.

"Uh, being yourself, the Messiah," he stammers. "You call yourself the Son of God, right?"

"Wouldn't it be cool if I was the Son of God?" you ask. "Haven't you people been waiting centuries for the Messiah to show up, reward the God's chosen righteous ones, and usher in a new era of peace and love?"

"Well…yes," another priest answers. "But not if it's going to be some glorified street magician like you, Jesus! You're not even a certified priest!"

You think for a second, then ask, "So then what do you people want from me?"

Turn to the NEXT PAGE

86

"Give us a sign, one that proves to everyone that you're really the Messiah," Ananus says, folding his arms smugly. "Maybe a sign straight from Heaven itself."

"Excuse me, but if Jesus proves that he is the Messiah, it'll confirm that you're all full of shit, right?" James #1 asks.

"I guess it will," Ananus replies. "But we're willing to take that chance."

"Ok, how's this for a sign?" you ask. "What year is it?"

"Thirty-two A.D.," Ananus says. "Everybody knows that."

"I don't," Philip says from somewhere behind you.

"Thirty-two A.D. is correct," you reply. "And how old am I? Thirty-two. We switched over from the B.C., or 'Before Christ,' calendar system to the A.D., or 'Adonis Domini' system, meaning 'Year of Our Lord,' on the exact day of my birth, which is December twenty-fifth. There's your damn proof. Booyah!"

"Not good enough," Ananus smirks. "We want something bigger, juicier, more supernaturalier."

All right, logic isn't going to get you anywhere with these idiots. Time to whip out the fireworks.

But should you summon a vision from Heaven or would it be more fun to give them a little taste of what Hell has to offer? It's no skin off your nose no matter which one you choose and you have a feeling that you're pretty much damned either way…

If you give them a sign from Hell, turn to PAGE 13

If you give them a sign from Heaven, turn to PAGE 128

"Everybody repeat after me. Num-num-num—" you start to say.

"We're not falling for that bullshit again, Jesus!" one skeletal teenager screams.

"Hey, aren't there some great restaurants in yonder city?" you ask.

"They're all closed," another woman answers, not amused. "The owners are out here, too, waiting for your sorry ass to feed us some food."

"Stop stalling!" another man calls out.

"Looks like I'm in a real pickle here," you mutter.

"Mmmm, pickles..." a starving child says, pawing listlessly at the ground.

You grit your teeth and hold the loaves and fishes up. It is deathly quiet, except for the sound of weeping women and groaning children.

You close your eyes and think about the Siamese twins. You tear the bread and fish in half, expecting the worst. Miraculously, though, the bread and fish keep multiplying every time you break them in half!

"Holy mackerel," someone mutters. "He's splitting mackerel."

It doesn't make sense to you and you've never seen such a thing before, but it's working, so you're going to run with it.

"Fish and bread for everybody!" you scream, tossing pieces of the food up in the air. "God must be letting me do whatever I please now!"

Your disciples start passing around armfuls of fish and bread. The multitude goes wild.

Everyone spends the next hour stuffing fish and bread into their mouths. When the food orgy is finally over, your disciples collect all the scraps and find that there are twelve baskets of fish and bread left over!

"Ok, no more food multiplication for today. People are starting to pack it up to take home with them," you say. "But I guess this takes care of our own food needs for the rest of our journey, boys."

"We won't have to steal dogs and cook them anymore!" Matthew rejoices.

"Mmm. I can't wait until Jesus gets his miracle-making hands on some nice steaks," James #2 says, licking his fat, greasy lips.

A chorus of satisfied burps and farts echo all around you. Everybody seems to be lazily, happily waiting for something else from you. Maybe now you should serve them up one of your famous speeches.

People start chanting, "Par-a-ble! Par-a-ble!"

A heaping platter of parables it is, then!

Turn to PAGE 23

Forget performing any more miracles tonight. And forget Judas and all the nefarious activities he's probably planning. You're hungry, and since you have a vague suspicion that you might not have many more meals left on this planet, you tell your disciples that you'd like to have your Last Supper at someplace cheap so you can totally pig out.

Your first choice, The Promised Land Café, is packed (because it's Senior Citizen's Night, of course) and it'll take forever to get a table.

Your second choice, Bethlehem's Big Buffet, is also full, but they lead your party to their barn out back and offer to let you all eat there.

The hostess dusts off an old manger and motions for you to sit in it. Three wise-looking gentlemen and a trio of shepherds look at you expectantly from across the room.

"Oh hell no! I'm not going through all this shit again," you pout.

You storm out of the barn and wind up settling for a lukewarm meal of lion burgers and fried locusts over at the fast food joint McDaniel's down the street.

Some Last Supper this turned out to be, you think.

Halfway through the meal, your disciples start speculating about who will betray you tonight, which has pretty much been the main topic of discussion at dinnertime since you first mentioned the betrayal.

"I won't name any names," you begin. "But I will tell you that he whoever dips his hand into this hummus dish with me, that is he who shall also betray me."

Nobody goes near the hummus for the rest of the dinner. Of course, you know that this was just a sneaky way for you to bogart all the hummus for yourself.

"Is it going to be me?" one of your disciples asks.

You do a double-take at him. "Who the hell are you? Do you even know me well enough to betray me?"

"That's Simon," James #1 says. "He's been with us for your entire ministry."

"Oh I get it! So there's a Simon *and* a Simon Peter..." you say.

"Forget those guys, Jesus," Philip calls out. "I'm the traitor. I just know it."

"No, it's not you, Philip," you answer. "And it's not you, Simon, although I'm not on familiar terms with you and have no reason to trust you at this point."

"Oh," Philip says disappointedly. "Well, I'll betray you if you want me to, Jesus."

"I said it's whoever dips into my hummus! Are any of you doing that right now?"

"I am—"

"No! No you're not, Philip! You're not even at the same table as me! You're sitting in the children's play area, so it's absolutely impossible for you to be doing that!"

Just then, Judas breezes in with another jug of wine.

"Whoa! Roasted red pepper hummus! Yoink!"

He dips his finger into the hummus bowl just as you dip your hand into it. There is an awkward silence.

"What?" Judas asks. "Did I hear the tail end of you saying something about someone betraying you tonight, Jesus? What kind of a boner-head would do something like that?"

"Duh," Philip says with a mouthful of lamb nuggets. "You."

Judas' eyes go wide as he looks at the hummus. His secret is out.

John breaks the ensuing silence. "You know, sometimes whenever I'm eating bread, I like to imagine it's your body, Jesus. And drinking wine is kind of like drinking your blood. Is that weird or what?"

"Gross…" both Jameses say in unison.

"I mean, I'm not obsessed with Jesus or anything," John says. "It's just something fun I like to do to help pass the time whenever Jesus isn't around, ok?"

You are simultaneously creeped out and flattered by this revelation, but John also just gave you an idea.

"Hey, if that's how Johnny Boy wants to remember me after I'm dead, then I think it's cool," you say, giving his tummy flab a couple of tickles. "As a matter of fact, I think all of you should do it."

You pick up a buttermilk biscuit and break it up into pieces. "Here. Take this buttery goodness into your mouths and think of it as my body. Go on. It's not gay or anything."

A majority of your disciples shoot embarrassed sideways glances at each other, but they eventually take some of the pieces and timidly nibble on them.

You pour some crimson fluid out of a wine jug. "And this wine—"

Judas interrupts. "Yo, can we wrap up this Last Supper thingy soon? I've got someplace to be."

You glare at him and continue. "Drink this wine and imagine that you're gulping down warm blood straight from my jugular vein. For I am the sacrificial Lamb of God."

Turn to the NEXT PAGE

You pass the cup around the table. Simon Peter takes a sip and starts gagging.

"Ugh! That's not wine! It's actual lamb's blood, Jesus," he says.

"Well then it's even more appropriate to what I'm saying," you retort.

"Wait! What about salad?" Tad asks. "Can we substitute a salad in remembrance of your body if we're, like, watching our carbs?"

"Yes, Tad, just make sure there are croutons on it," you answer, getting annoyed. "It can be crackers, wafers, toast - as long as there's a bread-like substance involved, it works."

"I like clam juice," James #1 says. "Can I drink that instead of wine or blood?"

"Guys, the point of this is that whatever you want to eat and whatever you want to drink, just think of those things as the body I'm giving and the blood I'm going to spill so that everyone's sins can be forgiven and everybody can go to Heaven! Write this down so other people will do it, too. And slap a catchy yet solemn-sounding name on it like 'The Final Meal' or 'Communion.' Oooh, I like that! Communion. There. Done. Have I made it clear enough?"

Your disciples assure you that they understand, although they spend the rest of the meal asking increasingly stupid questions that convince you otherwise. The whole time, Judas keeps checking his sundial and looking at the door like he's itching to get out of here.

The nerve of that guy. His impending betrayal is really starting to eat at you. You're *really* not looking forward to forgiving him for that. And you know what? Who says you even have to? Maybe *he* should be the one getting betrayed by *you*!

Whoa. You're thinking crazy thoughts…

Turning in your own formerly-loyal follower? You need to relax.

There's a beautiful garden in Gethsemene that you could go pray and meditate in. Yeah, that's the mature, Messianic thing to do in this situation, right?

If you pray in the Garden of Gethsemene, turn to PAGE 116

If you betray Judas, turn to PAGE 152

92

For some reason, you feel like preaching. You don't know where it comes from or why, but you've got all of this wisdom in your head and you need people to hear it. Judas and Bart got you all riled up.

So you gather your crew and head up Mount Sinai.

You ascend the ever-loving shit out of that mount until one of your sandals suffers a massive blow-out.

Tad offers to mend it. He's been dying to give you a shoe makeover, and this seems like a good place to stop anyway.

You turn and discover that hundreds of people are now gathered beneath you for some reason.

How did you not hear this multitude following you all the way up here? Weird. Guess you might as well say something to them.

"Hello!" you call out. "Y'all ready for some sermonizing, or what?"

You hear a few faint sounds of agreement. You clear your throat.

"Check this out, y'all. I call it 'The Beatitudes.' Here we go. Blessed are the rich, for their massive fortunes on earth will be multiplied tenfold in Heaven. Blessed are the beautiful and handsome, for they are superior to all the ugly people. Blessed are—"

"BOOOOO!!!" you hear from somewhere below.

You feel a tap on your shoulder. It's Matthew.

"Jesus, no offense, but I don't think the people like what you're saying. I mean, look at them. They're all hungry, downtrodden, poor in spirit, and really really meek. How about finagling your speech a little to pacify your audience?"

You pause and think on this for a second. "You're right. Thanks, Matt."

You turn back to the crowd.

"Uh, blessed are the middle class, for they live within their means, invest their earnings wisely, and shall have decent retirement funds to live off of in their golden years."

You are met with a sea of dull expressions. A few people in the back wander off, in search of a better sermon, no doubt.

Matthew shakes his head.

"You're getting close, man, but I think you're over-thinking this. Try just thinking of one undesirable human trait and then reward that trait with the opposite of it. Keep it simple and give 'em what they want to hear."

The crowd is restless, but you think you've got the hang of it.

"I'm sorry, everyone! That was some new material I wanted to try out, but it obviously needs some polishing. Here's the good stuff, though. Ahem. Blessed are the meek, for they shall inherit the earth."

"YAAAAAYYYY!!!!!!"

The crowd's cheers drown you out. When they quiet down, you continue.

"Blessed are the poor in spirit: for theirs is the kingdom of Heaven. Blessed are the merciful, for they shall obtain what else? Mercy!"

"WOOOHOOOO!!!!"

You're on a roll! You've got the whole world in your hands. You can say anything to these people.

Glancing back, you see Matthew busily writing everything down.

"And all you ugly people out there, God's gonna make you beautiful! Don't you light no candle and then stick it under no damn bushel tree! Put up that thing up on a big ol' candlestick so it can light up your whole mutha-fuckin' house! Can I get an 'amen,' my brothas?"

You don't get much applause for that one and it probably won't make it into Matthew's book, but whatever. You're having fun being the world's Messiah right now...

Turn to PAGE 25

94

"I think I've got a way out of this mess, boys," you say. "Tenus, you distract the crowd by moaning loudly and loosening your bowels. Meanwhile, I'll start swaying my cross back and forth until it tips over. I'll fall onto a group of soldiers, hopefully crushing one or two of them. Then I'll yank my arms free, steal a sword, and take one unlucky soldier hostage..."

Tenus nods weakly and you turn to Booba.

"Booba, you start twisting and twirling your cross down into the dirt like a drill until you're close enough to the ground to just hop off. We'll rendezvous at the foot of Tenus' cross, pull him down, and then split. Cool?"

"Ron day what?" Booba whispers.

"Forget it! It's a French word! Just go!" you yell.

Tenus lets out a pathetic cry and unleashes a torrent of foul diarrhea. The crowd gasps with delight and people start taking bets on when he will die, which is one of the most fun and exciting activities to do as a crucifixion spectator.

Now's your chance! You push back against your cross with all of your might. It moves with surprising ease and nobody seems to even notice what you're doing.

"It's working! It's really working!" you loudly whisper. But when you look over at Booba, your smile fades. The pain and stress of twisting his cross must have been too great for his weakened body and now he limply hangs there, dead.

Tenus watches you, his eyes wide with fear. The crowd seems to have lost interest in his gushing bowels and now you've rocked your cross beyond the point of stopping.

You lean way back, and as the momentum reverses, your cross creaks forward at great speed. You're going to land face-first onto a group of soldiers who look like they've been wise to your escape plan since the beginning. They probably were, actually, since everyone could hear you telling your brilliant plan to Tenus and Booba.

Oops.

Your last earthly sight is a soldier holding up his spear, the razor-sharp tip aimed right at the spot where your skull is going to be in half a second. Gee, who woulda—

THUNK!

THE END

You're hanging on a cross in front of a thousand bloodthirsty people. How could you possibly get out of this? By swinging your cross around until it falls down? Puh-lease!

There have been exactly zero crucifixion escapes. Ever. There hasn't even been anyone stupid enough to attempt it.

Let's face it—you're mortally wounded and you can barely think straight at this point. You may as well just give up the ghost. But it looks like it's going to be quite some time before that happens...

Assholes. Look at them pointing and laughing at your suffering. They don't deserve your redemption. Maybe you shouldn't give it to them. You could have the last laugh as their souls burn in Hell.

That might be a satisfying payback for all of your pain and misery.

"Oooh wee, this sucks," you groan.

The sky darkens with ominous clouds.

"Whoa. Did you just do that, Jesus?" Tenus asks, frightened.

"I don't know," you reply, confused. "Maybe my father up in Heaven did. I hope He sends us some rain. I'm so thirsty."

"The Jew King wants more drink?" a guard yells. "Get him one!"

Well now that's thoughtful of them, you think. Maybe the dark clouds scared a little fear into their hearts. Or maybe they're simply showing some grace and compassion on your pitiful ass. Perhaps it wouldn't be such a terrible thing to be humanity's savior after all.

The soldiers tie a big sponge to a pole and hold it up for you to drink. Should you accept this as a token of trust and goodwill? Or if you accept their offering, will you be validating the awful way that they've been treating you—the guy who's healed all their diseases and slept in ditches to give them an unconditional message of love and hope?

Maybe you should just skip the drink and die thirsty. Fuck this earthly body, fuck this planet, fuck all of God's crummy Creation.

If you take the drink, turn to the NEXT PAGE

If you refuse the drink and die, but without saving humanity, turn to PAGE 99

If you refuse the drink and die, but you want to save humanity, turn to PAGE 119

96

Sucker! This sponge is filled with vinegar, too! And probably piss and semen and whatever other vile fluids they could squirt onto it.

Those damn humans and their damn twisted sense of humor!

I can't believe you fell for that trick *again*! How could you be so stupid?

Even though you deserve some kind of nasty ending for making such a dumb choice, instead you're going to get some mercy (or perhaps further torture and anguish, depending on how you view this book) by letting you—

Turn back to PAGE 95 and don't choose this choice again!

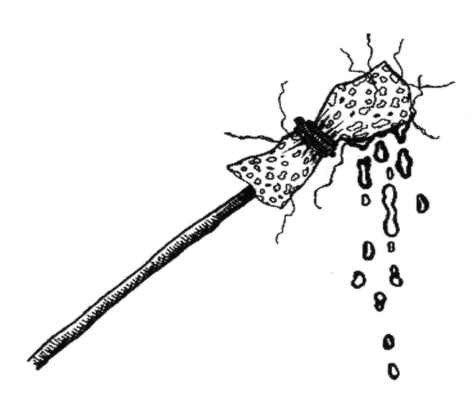

When you arrive at the whorehouse, you find a sign hanging on the door that reads, "CLOSED DUE TO SEVERE STONING OF OUR HARLOTS—WILL RETURN ONCE WE FIND SOME MORE HARLOTS."

This bums you out even further. You were really looking forward to saying woe unto all those darn whoremongers!

Just then, a strange-looking man rushes out of the house next door.

"Have mercy on my son, Jesus! He's only seven years of age and I fear that he's gone lunatic. Sometimes he falls into the fire, other times he falls into mud puddles."

"You really shouldn't leave those kinds of things lying around," you reply with a heavy sigh. "Go ahead. Take me to your fucked-up kid."

Minutes later, with one glance at the child, you confirm that he has, indeed, gone lunatic.

He sports a full-grown beard, produces a steady stream of pungent cheese from his navel button, and seems to take great pleasure in gnawing the heads off live chickens – fairly atypical behavior for a seven-year old child, even in this vulgar day and age.

Bartholomew suggests that the child could just be another victim of demonic possession.

Satan pokes his head through an open window and hisses, "Yeah. No shit, Shadrach…"

"Demons? Well that's easy enough to handle," you say. "I'll just exorcise him."

"Hey, you should know that I infest people with my demons for good reasons," Satan dryly says.

"Oh yeah?" you reply. "And what might those reasons be, Satan?"

"Those reasons are private to me," he says, his red face turning an even a deeper shade of red with anger. "And you won't always be around to keep casting them out of people, Jesus! What if something bad happens to you? What then? You think your little disciples will be able to do it?"

"Oh, get thee beneath me, Satan, and lick my holy scrotum," you say.

He climbs through the window and moves toward your crotch.

You hold up your hand and he stops in his tracks.

Turn to the NEXT PAGE

"Whoa! That was just a figure of speech," you tell him. "You don't have to obey every blessed word that comes out of my mouth."

"Really? God said you have absolute authority over me in Earth, Heaven, and Hell," Satan says. "Whew! You had me worried there for a second. I do *not* want to lick your balls."

But Satan did just raise an interesting point. Your disciples should be able to heal infirmities and exorcise demons in your name, especially since you won't be on Earth for long BECAUSE YOUR DAD SENT YOU ON A FREAKING SUICIDE MISSION!

Speaking of your imminent death, it's almost Passover and you've always wanted to visit Jerusalem during Passover before you die.

"You know, you're right, Beelzy. I think I might let my disciples handle this one. It's time that you guys learn how to cast demons out on your own. You've seen me do it enough times."

"Awww, Jesus!" Thomas whines. "We can't perform miracles! I don't even believe half the miracles I've seen you do!"

"Yeah, and my demon isn't even the real problem here," Satan gripes. "This guy's kid just so happens to be a weird, klutzy little creature. My demon's inside there, trying to earn a clean, dishonest living. He ain't hurting nobody."

"Demon or no demons, I can't handle this child anymore, Jesus," the boy's father cries. "All of his chicken head-biting is ruining my poultry farm!"

Enough already. No matter who ends up healing what, you're ready to shove off for Jerusalem.

These small towns with their small-town people and their small-town problems…you can deal with them when you've got more time in the infinite afterlife…

If you cure the child yourself, turn to PAGE 52

If you give him to your disciples to cure, turn to PAGE 110

Selfishly, you choose to die without offering humanity any salvation. Those ungrateful dickheads burned you one too many times, often literally, and they can all suffer in the Lake of Fire and Brimstone for all of Eternity with Satan for all you care.

So a few hours later, after all the bones in your body dislocate from their sockets and the last drop of blood drips out from one of your countless gaping wounds, you finally breathe your last breath, just another ordinary criminal crucified for doing something stupid in the eyes of the court.

However, this wasn't such a great choice for you to make because you've broken your covenant with God and now all of your spilled blood is going to be utterly meaningless.

The undertaker buries you in a simple, unmarked grave, and your disciples are severely confused and disappointed when you fail to return to life within the next week.

Soon, your disciples return home to the families whom they left behind all those months ago (those whose families haven't yet died from starvation or been sold in the underground sex slave market).

All of your adventures and the lessons that you taught are quickly forgotten, having never been published, guarded, and translated into other languages like they would've been if you were, you know, a true savior.

So Christianity never really gets off the ground, and without the healthy competition between it and all the other religions of the world, the notion of religion itself eventually falls by the wayside.

Surprisingly, future generations of the world turn out to be a lot more peaceful and productive because of this.

So in a roundabout way, you kind of did bring about peace on Earth.

Amen and what-not.

THE END

100

It's been a long time since you last blessed some children. Plus, you're tired of talking to adults today, so you lead your group over to the schoolhouse.

Dozens of kids are there enjoying recess when you arrive, and you wander through the busy play area touching random children and muttering generic blessings over them.

You lay a hand on one scraggly little kid's head and he starts screaming and bites your leg. Even through the thick fabric of your robe, the little bugger manages to draw blood.

A few older kids rush over, pull him away from you, and face you menacingly.

"What is this naughtiness I see, oh ye rebellious children? It is I, Jesus, come to bless you with God's eternal love."

"Eat serpent snot, Jesus!" a kid with a mohawk screams.

"Yo, you're on our turf now, prophet," another kid with a lot of piercings all over his face and body says. "We run everything that goes on around here and that includes dishing out blessings."

"You and all your homo disciples are a bunch of gay queer faggoty homos," a chubby kid sneers.

"Oh no, my ears did not just hear his dirty little trifling mouth say those words," Thaddeus says.

"You know, I ain't scared of ripping a child's head off its torso if it's deserving of that, Jesus," Thomas mutters.

Your other disciples bristle at the disrespectful little squirts, but you assure them that you've got this under control.

These kids are bad news for sure, but they're also so tough and cool that you can't help but secretly want to fit in with them.

"Looks like you kids have a nice little gang going here, huh?" you say with a friendly smile.

"Yeah we do! What's it to you, bitch?" the mohawk kid replies.

"We don't need no stupid fat adults like you nosing around in our business," the pierced kid says. "So why don't you scram before we chop your punk-ass balls off?"

You nonchalantly lift your eyebrows. "Tell me something. Any of you kids like throwing sticks at frogs?"

"Yeah, we do that sometimes. So what?" a scruffy-looking kid with one leg answers.

"Uh huh. I thought so. Me too," you say in your most suave tone of voice. "How about collecting donkey turds?"

"You bet we do!" the fat kid says. "I'll trade ya for some if ya gots any!"

You shoot a grin back at your disciples. You're totally on top of this situation.

"What's up your sleeve, JC?" Bart whispers to you through clenched teeth. "Let's leave. I smell bad publicity no matter what the outcome is here."

What Bart doesn't know is that you've got not one, but two sweet ideas up your sleeve right now. One for each sleeve, you might say.

Now that you've infiltrated the gang and earned their trust, you could probably ditch your disciples and join them without much trouble. Finally, you'll be part of the in-crowd.

But you could also send a message to all the other disobedient children of the world that they better respect Jesus Christ or face the unholy consequences...

Which choice gives you the bigger boner?

If you hang with the gang, turn to the NEXT
PAGE

If you rebuke the children for being little shits, turn
to PAGE 105

102

You turn around, hike up your robe around your hips, and flash your bare ass to your disciples.

"Later, losers! I'm hanging out with the cool kids from now on."

"But what about all your heaven-sent visions, Jesus?" John whimpers. "You're supposed to save our everlasting souls from damnation."

"Oh shut up. I'm not going to wait around for one of you fuck-faces to sell me out so I can go down like some kind of punk," you reply.

Your former apostles slowly walk away from you in disbelief.

Minutes later, you find yourself being warmly received by the youths in the gang, who like to call themselves 'The Rough n' Tumbles.'

That afternoon, they initiate you as a full-fledged member of their gang by making you jump into a filthy sewer hole for a full five minutes.

The next few years fly by in a whirlwind of fun and juvenile delinquency. Due to your healing skills, vast experience with living on the street, and other God-given supernatural abilities, you expand your gang's turf by another ten blocks and completely annihilate your rival gang, 'The Urchins from Ur.'

It's so cool to run around with the bad kids and do whatever you want, whenever you want—no responsibilities, no omnipotent father peeking over your shoulder every few seconds.

Everything is pretty sweet for a while. But once puberty sets in for the other guys, they start losing interest in the gang, and instead of hanging around you, they do lame things like overdosing on drugs, finding careers, and getting married.

You take over as the gang's leader and try to recruit some new blood to restore the gang to its former glory, but you're pushing forty years old now, and people from your time period and region of the world don't live for much longer than that.

One cold winter morning, you cough yourself to death in a random doorway in Jerusalem.

When the sanitation workers remove your body, they wonder why such a haggard, disgusting human being would die with a half-grin frozen on his face.

They don't understand that you died with a bittersweet smirk on your lips because, as you gasped for your last breath, you thought about how this was part of your plan all along—you've always lived on the streets and you always knew you'd die on them, too.

THE END

104

You decide to weather out the violent storm with heaping amounts of indifference.

You crawl back to your soggy corner of the boat's cabin and huddle there angrily until you eventually pass out. When you wake back up, half of your disciples have disappeared (washed overboard) and the awful tempest still rages on.

It continues nonstop like this for thirty-nine days and thirty-nine nights.

When the sky finally clears up, you don't see a hint of land anywhere. It's as if the entire world has been flooded, which it most certainly has.

Eventually, you starve to death, having eaten everything and everyone on the boat.

When your spirit ascends to Heaven, you angrily demand an explanation from God.

"Dad! Another flood? What the hell?" you cry.

God nonchalantly informs you that He had severe doubts about letting humanity redeem itself after all.

"So I decided to flood the whole damn thing and maybe start over in a little while. If I feel like it," He says. "And before you go quoting old scriptures at me, technically, because I only flooded Earth for thirty-nine days and nights this time, I'm still keeping my whole 'no-more-forty-day-floods rainbow promise thingy' that I made with that guy Noah so long ago."

"But I was just getting things cooking with my Christian ministry!" you scream at him, now in full-blown tantrum mode.

"Eh...things just weren't working out with you as a human. Humans suck. So I wiped them all out, along with all the other land-based creatures. Now it's just you and Me and lots and lots of fish, son," God says, stretching His legs and yawning dreamily. "I haven't figured out how to drown out all the water creatures yet. Maybe you could help Me brainstorm how to do that. We've got plenty of time."

Eternal life just got a lot less exciting.

THE END

"You kids like laughing at me, do ya?" you sneer. "How about I give you something funny to laugh about!"

With that, you start rebuking each and every one of those little fuckers by name.

ZOT!

A bolt of lightning zaps out of the empty sky and fries the kid with the pierced face.

All the childish laughter on the playground dries up real quick. The other kids scream and try to scatter, but their gloomy fates are sealed at this point.

A large boulder rolls across the field and crushes the Mohawked dude.

SQUISH!

You point at the chubby kid with your big toe and mummify him instantly.

FOOF!

Vipers swizzle up out of the ground and bite the remaining children before they can escape, and within the span of a minute, you have rendered the playground deadly quiet.

It dawns on you that you might not want anyone to keep a record of this particular incident.

"Uh...whoopsie," you say, blushing. "Did anybody happen to see me slaughter all of those arguably innocent schoolchildren?"

"Not me, Jesus," John says quickly. "I was, uh, looking at that grass over there while you were smiting the youths."

"I haven't been able to see past my beard in weeks," Matthew mumbles and you notice that his entire face is indeed one big overgrown mass of matted hair.

Simon Peter's assistant Mark also pretends that he didn't witness your terrible violent overreaction, and you completely ignore whatever the hell Simon tells you that he saw.

Well, looks like that takes care of that potentially embarrassing legend spreading around to any of your prospective believers!

Now if you could just get your loyal disciples to look you in the eye again.

"You...you're starting to spin out of control, JC," Bart says sadly. "I've never seen you rebuke anyone like that."

Turn to the NEXT PAGE

106

You know Bartholomew is right. Lately your powers have become more and more erratic.

Maybe it's because of all the faith that your new believers have in you. Have you grown too powerful, too fast?

Something's not right in your head. You feel all out of sorts. You're so damn famous and everyone expects so much from you. You give and you give and sometimes you wonder when it'll be someone else's turn to do some giving around here...

"Watch it, Jesus! For Christ's sake, chill out, man!" James #1 screams. "Look what you're doing to Bart!"

You look over and see that you were so lost in thought that you've shriveled Bart's hand down to a tiny little nub. You apologize and restore it to its previous half-withered size.

"You need to loosen up, big guy," John says. "How about a two-hour back rub from yours truly?"

"Oooh! Or a full-body rub," Tad suggests. "Like, the lower front, penis-shaped part of your body, specifically."

"Hey, Tad's comically overt sexual advances toward Jesus have given me a great idea!" Judas exclaims. "Since you're in such a foul, cursing mood, Jesus, as opposed to a kind, blessing mood, how about we head over to that whorehouse and you can say 'Woe' to all the pimps and whoremongers we find there?"

Hmmm...This day can't get much darker for you, so you might as well ruin the day for a bunch of hookers and other assorted lowlifes.

"Better late than never," you answer. "Lead the way, boys!"

You follow your followers off in the direction of the whorehouse...

Turn to PAGE 97

You tell the crowd that you're done healing for the day, that their diseases will all still be here tomorrow, and that you'll heal them then.

Since it's the Sabbath and there's nothing to do in town, you wander around the outskirts for a while until you and your disciples happen upon a huge cornfield. In your usual 'free love and anything goes' fashion, you stroll amongst the cornstalks as if you owned the land yourself.

"Arrr! I be so hungry now, Jesus!" Andrew complains while stepping on a fresh ear of corn and crushing it beneath his fisherman's boots.

"Yeah, Jesus, we're positively starving! What ever are we to do?" Thaddeus groans, lazily swatting at the dozens of corn kernels that keep falling off the stalks onto his head.

Indeed, you haven't eaten all day and your tummy is growling something fierce. You stop in your tracks, noticing that you are in the middle of roughly a million corn plants. You watch a nearby scrawny raven picking at the corn and eating it.

An idea hits you.

Shooshing your disciples, you crouch down and sneak toward the raven. You lunge at it, but alas, it outmaneuvers you and takes flight, leaving you grasping at nothing but the worthless ears of corn that it was pecking at.

"Ah! This stupid corn got in the way of me scoring us a raven to cook up for some food!" you lament.

You start throwing a tantrum, biting at the corncobs and spitting kernels everywhere. A single corn kernel happens to land in Philip's mouth, which is perpetually agape because he's an utter simpleton.

"Yum! Corn taste good!" Philip smacks.

"Hey!" a man's voice calls out. "We see what you're doing!"

The priests that you encountered in town earlier start filing out from behind a cluster of cornstalks and rush toward you.

"You're that Jesus guy! We've been watching you, buster!" one of the high priests says. "You can't be picking and eating corn on the Sabbath. That's considered work and that's against the Holy Law! We're going to tell the even higher priests about this!"

Another priest pipes up, "We saw you healing all those people earlier, but we let you off the hook with that shit. But you've gone too far now."

Damn religious nuts. Think fast.

Turn to PAGE 40

"Verily, verily," you begin as you hold up the bread in front of the salivating throng. "This bread is my body. Eat of it and be whole!"

So far, so good, you think.

You lift up the smelly fish in your other hand.

"And this…fish…is my…blood? Drink it and remember me!"

"Huh? How the fuck are we supposed to drink a fish?" a man asks, instantly outraged.

Uh-oh, you think.

"Less speech and more eats!" someone yells from the back of the crowd.

"I thought you people would appreciate the symbolism I'm using here. It's all metaphors and what-have-you."

"We don't have nothing," a woman grumbles.

"Well…the fish is a metaphor for wine, which is a metaphor for my spilled blood, which is a metaphor for your path to Heavenly salvation," you stammer. "I'm your savior, you see?"

"Mmmm…a mouthful of fresh bloody fish guts sounds pretty good right about now," one man says, salivating heavily.

They're not even listening to you anymore, unable to see past their intense hunger.

"Um, maybe if we actually had some wine up here for illustrative purposes, this analogy would work better," you say uneasily. "Anybody? No? Look, I'm trying to make do with what I've been given here, people. Gimme a break."

"No, Jesus. You give us a break," another crazy-looking man says. "As in, break me off a piece of that fish you've got there!"

"Wait!" you cry. "I can save you all! Just give me some time—"

"We don't need no salvation!" a woman interrupts you. "We need food in our empty gullets!"

The screaming crowd surges forward and swarms over you, fighting over the scraps of food in your hands.

Moments before hundreds of scrambling feet crush your skull, you think, *So technically, this really wasn't my last supper, which would make the official Last Supper of Christ whatever I ate last night—that stale pita bread and those tough, stringy chicken kabobs. That's pretty depressing and unimpressive. I wonder if anyone documented it—*

THE END

One by one, your disciples lay hands on the child and attempt to cast the demon out of him.

But the kid isn't having any of that—floating around the room, biting whoever's closest, and flinging feces at the others.

Satan watches the mayhem unfold and roars with laughter from the corner of the room.

"Sorry, Jesus," Tad whines. "I'm all about a good shit-flinging when it's appropriate, but now is not the time or the place. We just can't exorcise this little fucker!"

"I say we slit his throat and be done with it," Thomas says, fingering his knife handle.

The other disciples murmur their agreements.

"What a bunch of faithless, idiots," you huff. "All you need is faith the size of a mustard seed and you could move mountains!"

"How big is a mustard seed?" Philip asks.

"Extremely tiny," you snap. "The smallest thing ever."

"Uh…a grain of sand is smaller than a mustard seed," Thomas snorts.

"No way," Simon Peter says. "A gnat's ass is the smallest thing in the world."

"If you guys doubt me in this matter, by all means, prove me wrong," you defiantly say.

Thomas borrows a mustard seed from the child's father while John chases down and catches a gnat.

After exhaustively comparing the seed to the gnat's ass, you see that Simon Peter is indeed right after all.

"Ha! He's right and you're wrong, Jesus!" Satan chides from across the room. "Infallible and all-knowing my hairy red goat-ass…"

"Well if Simon Peter's going to cheat and use a HUGE mustard seed and the teeniest little malnourished skeleton of a gnat, then yeah, of course he's right!" you pout. "But I swear upon the Virgin Mary's future grave that I could find a mustard seed that's smaller than that gnat's ass that you've got right there!"

"You do *that* and I'll actually start believing you're the Messiah," Thomas grunts.

They want to play this game, do they? Oh you'll play…

Without another word, you rush out of the house, purchase a large sack of mustard seeds, and start frantically comparing seed after seed to the gnat's ass in hopes of proving your point.

You get so caught up in this futile quest, that you completely forget about the possessed child running amok in the man's house and you spend the rest of the day searching for a mustard seed that can dwarf the size of the gnat's posterior.

What starts out as a curious argument soon turns into a life-long obsession as you and the gnat travel the world, searching for the smallest mustard seed, collecting other tiny objects, and keeping a detailed, miniscule record of them written on a single grain of rice.

Years later, as the world's oldest living person at the grizzled age of fifty-eight, you stop sifting and sorting through a large sand dune in the Sahara desert and reminisce about the wild and crazy life you led way back in your early thirties.

A single tear races down your dirty, weathered cheek, and you address the hot, lonely wind, "I coulda been a real somebody, you know. A legend. Instead, all I've got to show for my life are a handful of barely visible possessions and a few fuzzy memories. Why oh why didn't I just take one second and exorcise that stupid kid myself when I had the chance?"

The wind blows in the ensuing silence and you could swear that it sounds just like your old adversary's laughter.

What was his name?

Oh yeah…Satan.

Wonder what he's up to these days…

THE END

112

The following day, while passing through a small village, you are somewhat violently accosted by a strange man who charges up to you and shakes his fists in your face.

"Jesus Herbert Christ, you filthy son of a bitch!" he shouts. "You owe me a new pecker!"

"Excuse me?" Thomas says, drawing his knife and brandishing it toward the man menacingly. "You better explain yourself, fella, before you get gutted like a pig."

You wave Thomas away and kindly address the man, "I'm sorry, my good man. Do you feel that I have wronged you in some way, specifically relating to your genitalia?"

"Uh huh. Look at this shit," the guy grunts, lifting his robe to reveal a bloody, heavily-bandaged crotch.

Oof! Your disciples all grimace at the sight and instinctively grab at their own crotches to make sure everything is in its right place.

The guy drops his robe and continues, "I heard you give a speech back in Galilee and you said, 'If your right hand offends you, cut it off. And if your right eye offends you, pluck it out.' You remember saying all that bullshit?"

"Yes," you answer. "I've given that exact sermon dozens of times. Always a big crowd pleaser. Not really meant for the kiddies, though."

The man nods.

"Well after that, everybody started chopping off their hands and poking out their eyeballs, and I realized that I've been wasting too much time watching pretty girls and tugging on my dingus, so I did what you told me to and I cut that offensive pecker right off with an old rusty shovel yesterday," the man says. "But that's just made everything even worse! I still look at women all the time and now when I get all horny-like, I can't do nothing about it! So the way I figure it, you owe me a brand new wienie."

"Why don't you get lost, bozo?" Judas says. "Jesus uses a lot of figurative language in his sermons. It's not his fault that you took his message too literally and now you're a dickless eunuch."

Just then, your nose catches a familiar whiff of brimstone and Satan pops his head out from behind a nearby wall.

"Oooh! Sounds like you've got quite a eunuch, I mean unique, problem on your hands, Jesus!" Satan giggles.

"Um, who is this stupid-looking red person and why is he all up in our business?" Thaddeus snips.

"Guys, this is Satan, also known as the fallen archangel Lucifer," you sigh. "He rules Hell, tempts everyone to sin all the time, and makes sure there's always a surplus of hate, evil, and chaos in the world. Satan, these are my loyal disciples. Please don't make me go through all dozen or so of their names right now."

Satan and your apostles engage in a flurry of bows, curtsies, and hand-shaking with one another.

"Excuse me! Can we get back to Jesus fixing my disfigured dickhole, or what?" the eunuch cries.

"Oh, my bad. Allow me to put my petty life and friends and enemies on hold to help out this poor gentleman who purposefully, needlessly mutilated himself," you say, sarcasm dripping from every word.

"Thanks," the eunuch replies, ignoring your sarcasm. "By the way, when you fix my cock up, do you think you could you add a little girth to it? You know, as compensation for all my pain and suffering..."

"Well, sometimes my miracles aren't all that accurate. So it'll probably be more like a very circumcised version of your old penis," you reply.

"Eh, I'll take whatever ya got," the man says. "As long as I can pee out of it."

Taking a deep breath, you shove your hand up under the guy's robe, lay your hand lightly on his mangled pubic area, and for the first time in your ministry, you close your eyes to pray a prayer for complete genital restoration.

"Oh, I can't wait to penis...I mean, see this!" Satan cackles.

Turn to PAGE 140

"All right, everybody, form a single-file line over there," you say, resolved to heal the entire cursed, leprous lot.

The trembling crowd sends up a chorus of happy grunts and animal-like shrieks of delight as they shuffle their stiff, twisted limbs and attempt to arrange themselves into a straight line.

You take a deep breath and slowly reach out to the first leper, touching him lightly on the shoulder. You concentrate deeply and command him to be healed.

The withered man's body starts to shake under your hand.

"I think it's working!" you shout excitedly.

"Naw, I'm actually just having a seizure. Sorry 'bout that," the man says, his shaking becoming even more pronounced. "I gets the shakes when I don't gets my wine in the morning..."

"Hmmm, I'll try to heal you a little harder this time," you say, tightening your grip on him. "How about now? Do you feel whole, my son?"

"Hole? Yeah, I gots a big ol' hole in my cheek," he answers, pulling some rags down and pointing to a huge, open wound in the side of his face.

"Bless your heart, my child. Is that from the leprosy?" you ask him, genuinely intrigued.

"No. I fell on a stick with my face," he replies with a dumb grin.

Hmm...something's not right with this guy. You start mentally preparing yourself for a major disappointment any second now.

"I think we're wasting our time here, Young Jeezy," says Bartholomew. "Maybe you don't know how to heal leprosy yet. No biggie. You'll eventually figure it out and we'll come back and heal them later. If it gels with the rest of your schedule, of course."

"Yeah, let's blow this shithole, Jesus," Thomas says. "Nobody'll ever know."

"Nooooo," a one-legged man wails. "We'll knoooow..."

"Wait a minute, everybody," you say. "I think I've got this figured out. Has anyone here ever been diagnosed with leprosy, like, by an actual practicing doctor?"

The raggedy men look at you blankly.

"Whoever has leprosy, raise your hand," you say.

Nobody moves.

"Or raise what's left of your hand."

Still nothing.

"Or just raise anything you can."

The one-legged man falls over with a loud thud.

"I knew it. This isn't a leper colony after all – it's just a collection of disgusting imbeciles," you sigh. "And I can't heal grossness or stupidity. They're not real afflictions."

"But Jessusssth!" one man bellows.

"What?" you reply.

"Nothin'. I justh like thayin' your name," he says with a gap-toothed grin.

"I love these people," Philip says. "Can we please live here with them forever and ever?"

"I'm noting this down as an official healing incident because technically, Jesus did identify a problem and effectively solve it," Matthew says.

"You put whatever tickles your fancy in that little book of yours," you tell him. "Come on, boys. I'm in the mood to heal some major infirmities now. Let's ride. And by 'ride' I of course mean 'walk.'"

"Aw, I don't wanna go!" Philip grumbles. "These are my friends."

"Philip does pretty much fit right in around here," John says. "Let's allow him to stay if he wants to."

"No," you boldly command. "We've all been through too much together. You are my twelve apostles and we have many more mild adventures to share together. Giddyup!"

You exit the village of hopeless idiots and head off to Galilee. The two Jameses have to drag the reluctant Philip along behind you.

Three minutes later, however, Philip's already forgotten about leaving all of his sub-mental brethren behind and he's happily sniffing and laughing at his own farts like usual...

Turn to PAGE 42

116

The night is silent and peaceful. Even in the dim moonlight, you can make out all the vibrant colors of the garden's flowers and they seem to help calm your nerves a bit.

"Oh my God, I just *love* this garden!" Tad says, ruining the quietude. "It's such a great place for men to secretly meet up with other men on lonely nights like this."

"Hey, no offense, guys," you start. "But I need some peace and quiet right now so I'm going to pray over yonder in the Silent Prayer Rocks Area. Cool?"

"Jesus, wait!" Simon Peter grabs your arm. "I feel awful about what you said about me a while back. Am I really going to deny you three times?"

"Before the cock crows thrice, yes," you reply. "Or no, it's when the cock crows once, you deny me thrice. Yeah, that's it. My point is, you'll be a pussy before the cock gets up."

"I would never deny my savior, regardless of how many cocks crow however many times," he says sadly. "I bet you ten shekels I don't even deny you once."

"You're on, old friend," you reply with a smile.

You share a tender moment of friendly feelings for each other and then you head off alone to pray.

You kneel down in front of a large Prayer Rock, your knees instantly getting bruised up and sore on the small, jagged Prayer Rocks.

Why can't they have something softer than rocks to pray upon around here, you think. You should tell the guys to write that down as a rule somewhere – all churches and prayer centers should have comfortable praying surfaces available in them.

You close your eyes, clasp your fingers, and pray: "My Father, who's up in Heaven…this is really fucked up, ya know? I expected better from You, I guess. I know You sent me down here to forgive all the past, present, and future generations of mankind for their sinful, disgusting ways, but do I *really* have to get executed like this? Do You know what they do to criminals these days? It's barbaric. Is it too late for me to throw some other ideas out there to You?"

Your prayer is interrupted by the sound of a cock crowing nearby.

"Nice try, Simon Peter," you call out. "But it's way too early for a cock to be crowing."

"Dammit!" you hear Simon Peter loudly whisper from somewhere in the darkness.

"Easiest ten shekels I've ever made," you say with a chuckle. "Now where were we? Oh yeah, about this Messiah business…"

Just then, one of the Prayer Rocks moves under your knees. You look down to see that it's not a rock at all, but a turtle!

The turtle sticks its head out of its shell and says, "Pssst! Jesus! It's me, God!"

"Dad? Why are You a turtle?"

"I heard your prayers and I wanted to come down and answer your questions, but I can't just yell them down from Heaven like I normally do, you know?" the turtle whispers. "It's nighttime and I can't wake up all of Creation just because you're feeling inquisitive."

"You could've been something cool, like a deer or a tiger. Even Satan knew to take the form of a snake when he talked to Eve back in the Garden of Eden," you say, rolling your eyes. "See, that's my problem with You, Dad. I don't think You really understand life on Earth very well."

"Look here, Junior. I also could've sat up on My glowing ass in My heavenly throne room like I've done for the past few millennia and not even gotten involved in all the mess happening on this Me-forsaken planet! How about them apples?"

"I'm sorry. Forget it, Dad. We can argue about that later, I guess. So You've got some answers for me?"

"Yeah, but we've got to make this quick," the turtle says. "Any second now, Judas is going to show up with an angry mob to arrest you."

"Sheesh. Ok. Well, I have about a thousand questions," you whisper back. "Firstly, why can't I remember my life in Heaven before I became a human? Also, what do people do up in Heaven all the time? Is it just one never-ending worship-fest for You? And when people call us the Holy Trinity, I kinda understand what You and I are. We're dudes. But what's the Holy Spirit? Is it a chick? Or a bird-like organism? Like, are we having a threesome kind of thing? That's a pretty weird activity for a son to participate in with his father, don't You think? Dad? Hello?"

You look over and see that the turtle is slowly crawling away from you. He's making surprisingly good time, too, for a turtle.

Just then, you hear what sounds like an angry mob marching through the garden in your direction!

Peeking over your Prayer Rock, you see that yes indeed, it is an angry mob—civilians, high priests, and soldiers—complete with torches and swords.

Yikes!

And Judas proudly leads them right toward your praying spot!

Turn to the NEXT PAGE

That traitorous bastard! Your vision was right all along!

Of course it was right. They're always right. Except for your occasional visions of you cuddling with beautiful women. When are those visions going to start coming true? Probably never now that you're about to get lynched and become a martyr for the world...

While you have time, you should say goodbye to your disciples. You slink off the Prayer Rocks and quietly trot over to the spot where you left them. Not surprisingly, they've all fallen asleep.

Man, am I gonna miss these goofy knuckleheads, you think as you watch their peaceful slumbering. It's a shame you won't get to see them spreading your gospel unto all four corners of the one and only continent in this crazy, mixed-up, flat world.

But maybe there is a way to do just that. Judas and his flock haven't seen you yet and your disciples are all zonked out. Maybe you could hide in this garden until daylight, cut your hair and shave your beard off in the morning, and trade clothes with a shepherd or something.

You could create a whole new identity for yourself!

After a few months, everyone will assume you've either been eaten by wolves or fallen into a sinkhole. They'll call off the manhunt and that asshole Judas will have to repay his thirty pieces of silver for betraying you!

Then, you could find your disciples, all of whom will be running a wildly successful ministry based upon your teachings and poignant life stories, and together you could construct a real zinger of a Jesus Christ martyrdom legend to start passing around.

It's positively foolproof.

Or you could lie down with your disciples and wait for the Pharisees to come murder you.

Tough call.

If you hide out in the garden and enact your brilliant plan, turn to PAGE 22

If you lie down like a wussy and wait for death to come, turn to PAGE 124

"I'm not falling for that one twice, no matter how thirsty I am."

That's what you say, but nobody hears you say it because they're shoving the sopping wet sponge into your mouth again. Yep. Rancid vinegar with a hint of ass juice.

But whatever. You're over it, too tired to care anymore. You look left and right and see that Tenus and Booba have either yielded up their ghosts or they're catching cat-naps in between the shockwaves of pain.

The crowd continues jeering you. Boy, these fuckers can jeer like nobody's business…

"I couldn't possibly be more forsaken than this," you croak.

Just then, you hear a familiar coo and fluttering of wings, followed by the unpleasant sensation of bird claws digging deep into your scalp.

"That you, Perchy, old pal? You wouldn't forsake me, would ya?"

Perchy the dove grunts and a warm dribble of bird shit plops onto the top of your head and runs down your face.

"Awww! Not you too, Perchy!"

Perchy scratches around in your hair and pecks at your skull, apparently making a nest inside of your thorny crown, which had never occurred to you as being a really nice bird nesting zone.

You look up toward Heaven and cry, "Ok, God. You win. You're the Grand Forsaker, all right? You have forsaken the shit out of me. This is the most awesome forsaking that the world has ever witnessed. Until the end of time, there shall be no greater forsaker of sons in all of Creation. I'm finished. I'm forsook. Kaput. Bada-bing-bada-boom."

With that, your head drops and the world starts to fade out…

You feel your soul rise up and out of your mangled body. You float all the way up to Heaven. It takes quite a long time as Heaven is a lot further away than you expected and you don't know how to float faster.

When you finally get there, God is dancing around on the streets of solid gold and all the angels are celebrating your arrival with lots of singing and music-making on puffy white clouds. It's a pretty fruity scene.

"Well how about that?" you say aloud. "This place really *is* real and I *am* the Son of God. I wasn't crazy after all!"

"Well done, son," God says. "You did it!"

"Yeah, about that, Pops," you say. "What did I do exactly?"

"You died for humanity's sins, ushering in a new route to Heaven. No more nasty animal sacrifices and weird, primitive traditions. I don't know why I demanded all that crap in the first place. I also don't know why I created the concept of sinning…or Satan…or Hell."

Turn to the NEXT PAGE

120

"But Dad, this new plan of Yours is kind of…stupid. What if the humans don't buy it?"

"Then they can go to Hell with that butthole Lucifer!" God screams, causing all of Heaven to tremble to its very core. "They've got no choice in the matter. Plus, your disciples are going to convince the rest of the world to adopt My new system, which requires them to learn a whole new set of weird (yet blood-free, thanks to you) rituals."

You hilariously spit out the ambrosia that you were just sipping.

"What?!? You're really going to trust those half-wits? I'm not sure they're the most competent guys to lay the foundation of a new religion."

"I prefer to think of it not as a new religion, but more as a major spiritual overhaul. A do-over. And they'll be fine. Look, I want you to relax for a couple of days. You deserve a break. Go skinny-dipping with some seraphim, smoke out with the Holy Spirit, stuff yourself with some manna, maybe go watch one of my billion other inhabited planets. Then, when you're all rested up, I want you to go back to Earth to check up on your disciples and make sure they understand all the little things…like how I want Armageddon to go down and such."

"Armageddon? I never preached about that! Was I supposed to?"

"Chill. It's just the end of the world. I'll brief you on it later."

"I had no idea that was part of the plan."

"Neither did I until I thought of it just now."

"But what about Your eternal love and understanding?"

"You're trying My infinite patience, little man," God says, His brow furrowing. A couple of angels signal to you that you're treading on dangerous ground here.

A mini-vacation sounds good, but you're not sure you like where all of this is going. Should you question God's intentions and actions some more or should you just forget it and go party like it's 99 A.D.?

If you keep pressing God about His Master Plan for the universe, go to PAGE 123

If you shut up and obediently follow His orders, turn to PAGE 134

It's been a long month and you figure that it's about time to just walk away from your crazy life for a while.

So you push past Zaccheus, the Pharisees, and everyone else to embark on a nice, peaceful fishing trip...alone. Like always, your disciples tag along, though.

A few hours later, you feel a tug on your reel. A strong tug. You pull with all of your might, enlisting the very fat James #1 and James #2 to help you haul in what feels like a goat-sized fish.

But when Thomas leans over the boat to grab it, he bursts into laughter and lifts up a puny fish the size of a hamster. What the heck?

When he hefts it into the boat, you kick the tiny fish in anger. Your toe crumples painfully like you've just kicked a boulder.

"Ow! Holy mother of me that hurt!" you scream and bend down to look at your foot.

As the fish flops around and gasps for water, a coin plops out of its mouth. It's a shiny five-dollar piece!

You grab the slimy fish and it's way heavier than you thought. You hear some tinkling and realize it's burping out even more coins.

The other disciples gather around you and marvel at the growing pile of coinage.

"That fish just puked up roughly six pouches of coins, our adjusted gross tax liability!" Judas exclaims.

"It's a miracle!" someone cries.

"And a really dumb one at that!" someone else cries even louder.

"Let's head back to Jericho to nip this tax problem in the bud," you say proudly. "But while we're here, let's enjoy some fresh sushi!"

You joyously butcher the fish and consume its raw flesh with some rice, seaweed, and soy sauce.

Later, the Pharisees nervously stew about as you plop your coin pouches down onto the tax collector's table. He gives you a thumbs up.

"That Jesus is simply untouchable," the Pharisees whisper to each other.

"Not true," a hobbled old woman replies. "I touched the hem of his robe just last Tuesday and he healed my goiter right off my body!"

"Awww, shaddup!" Ananus yells at her, pushing her into a nearby sewage ditch.

But you don't see or hear any of this because you and your disciples are skipping down the street, looking for the next big thrill...

Turn to PAGE 35

122

You give in to Thomas' unwavering logic and place the coca leaves in the water, adding a generous amount of sugar cane. You serve the strange brown syrupy liquid to several guests, and soon enough, your new concoction is the hit refreshment of the wedding!

Most people find it mildly energizing and there are even reports that it seems to cure minor ailments such as headaches and botulism.

You dub the drink Christ Cola™ and form a partnership with Thomas, foregoing your ministry and selling your delightful beverage until the day you both die.

On your deathbed, you pass on the drink's secret recipe to your son, Harry Christ, and he promises to do the same for the son that he will surely begat one day. The recipe will remain largely unchanged for millennia to come.

Later, your great-great-great-great-great-great-grandson will learn how to carbonate the beverage, making it fizzy and fun. Then his great-great-great-great-grandson will learn how to replace the sugar cane with a much cheaper and sweeter refined corn syrup, forever sealing the destiny of your life's work in the cups and mouths of the world's thirsty nations.

Sure, there will be imitators who arise from time to time, claiming to have the same sweet flavor and pleasant aftertaste as Christ Cola, but the truth-seekers will always know the difference. Even your derivative beverages like Diet Holy Sprite™ and Heavenly Father's Root Beer™ fly off the shelves. Your famous soda will even outlast several other brands in the Great Cola Wars of the late twentieth century. Good for you!

So you wound up living the life of a non-alcoholic beverage tycoon. It could be worse. At least you didn't inspire centuries of needless religious warfare that claimed millions upon millions of human lives. Now you're just indirectly responsible for billions of humans dying from Type II Diabetes…

THE END

"One last question, Father," you start. "Why would You enforce such a crappy, convoluted spiritual arrangement? If You love all these silly humans You created, and You want to hang out with them in Heaven for Eternity, why make them jump through so many hoops to do that? It's all so sloppy and frankly...imperfect."

God looks at you intently for a moment. You can hear the tiniest baby angel queefing in its cloudy crib miles and miles away.

That's how quiet Heaven is right now.

"What can I say, son?" God replies. "I work in mysterious ways."

"Really? That lame-ass hoodwink of an umbrella justification, that's really Your answer, Pop? And that's why I just took the form of a human for thirty years and died a senseless, mortifying, agonizing death?"

God looks at you and doesn't say a damn thing.

"What about Satan?" you say, raising your voice just a little too much. "How about I go kill *that* guy? Give me a couple of your toughest archangels and I bet we could just put this whole good versus evil thing to rest right now."

"*You* don't get to question *Me!*" God booms at you.

You can feel that God's ultimate wrath is stretching the fabric of reality to its limit right now. One more push and He might just tear all of Creation apart and start over.

You throw your hands up in defeat.

"Sheesh! Settle down, Big Guy. Ok, ok. I'll toodle around up here for a couple of Earth days. Then You and I can have a pow-wow about the End Times, and I'll head back down to Earth and smooth everything over with any of my ex-disciples that I can find. Are we cool?"

You spread your arms out for a hug.

"For now I suppose, yes," God glowers, giving you a weak, shallow hug.

"Good good. For the record, next time we're going to create Creation, I want some more input. I've got some ideas on how to streamline some things—"

God clears His throat, obviously perturbed. On Earth, the oceans rise a few feet and a thousand people drop dead in Corinth for no discernible reason.

You decide that maybe it's time you just shut up like a good, obedient son and party your righteous dick off like your Holy Father instructed you to do...

Turn to PAGE 134

You lie down and pretend to be sleeping.

Minutes later, the mob arrives and noisily surrounds you.

You crack your eyes open a tiny bit and see that, oddly enough, the noise doesn't appear to have roused any of your disciples from their sleep, except for Philip, who's always been a light sleeper.

"Keep it down, Jesus," Philip yawns. "Pray quieter or something."

"Now remember, men," Judas calls out. "Whoever I kiss, that's the guy who thinks he's the Messiah and that's who you need to arrest!"

At this, Thaddeus sits bolt upright and puckers his lips, his eyes expectantly shut tight.

"Lay it on me, big boy!" he says to the darkness.

Judas walks right past him to your spot, kneels down, and plants a big wet one right on your forehead.

"End of the line, old chum," he whispers into your ear.

"Huh?" you say, feigning sleepiness. "Sorry, mister. Me no speaky Aramaic."

Judas sighs and snaps his fingers.

A couple of guards roughly yank you up from the ground, restraining your arms and patting you up and down for weapons.

By now, all of your disciples are sitting or standing, except for Simon Peter, whose face is now suspiciously covered up as if he doesn't want to be recognized by Judas and the soldiers. He snores loudly, forcefully.

Even in his sleep, he denies being associated with me, you think.

"He's clean," the guard grunts after he pats you down from head to toe. "Filthy as an unbathed leper, actually, but clean of any weaponry."

"Good," croons the high priest Ananus, strutting forward from the midst of the mob. "Well done, good and faithful servant Judas. Come to me and collect your handsome reward."

Ananus proceeds to slowly, carefully count out thirty pieces of silver into Judas' palm. Judas makes him count it twice, gloating over the final sum both times.

"Thirty whole pieces of silver! I'm rich! I can finally pay off all my gambling debts, find a real job, and start living an honest, respectable life," Judas says. "I knew this apostle business would pay off for me eventually!"

Judas high-fives a few soldiers and dances a little victory jig.

"Nice knowing ya, Jesus," he continues. "And as for the rest of you disciple guys, I know you might hate me right now, but once all this betrayal-of-our-lord-and-savior awkwardness blows over, don't hesitate to look me up sometime in Thessalonica! Ciao!"

With that, Judas scurries off into the night, never to be seen again.

Just then, Thomas whips out his trusty dagger.

"You dirty sonsabitches!" he screams. "You'll never take any of us alive!"

Before anyone can react, he takes a swipe at one of the guards who's holding you, slicing his ear clean off of his head.

Everyone is shocked for a moment, then all hell breaks loose with disciples, priests, and guards all shouting and holding blades toward one another in menacing fashions.

This is bad. But even though you're severely outnumbered, you and your men might be able to overpower the mob and find out who's really trying to kill you.

Or maybe if you heal the poor soldier's ear, the high priests will feel sorry for you and let you off the hook this time.

Then again, this could be God's subtle way of telling you to sneak away and regroup like you could've done a few minutes ago…

If you heal his ear like a true, benevolent Messiah would, turn to the NEXT PAGE

If you finish the job Thomas started and turn this into a bloodbath, turn to PAGE 150

If you make use of John's diversion and flee the scene, turn to PAGE 158

"Now now…we don't cut, Thomas. You know better than that," you sternly say, reaching over to regenerate the guard's ear.

"Wow! Thanks, Jesus," the guard cries, his ear fully restored. "Guess I've got an extra ear now! What good luck for me!"

He bends down and picks up the ear that John cut off and slips it in his pocket.

"Not so fast, Christ. I'm onto you. You're trying to bribe us!" Ananus cries, grabbing another guard's sword.

He effortlessly chops off the guard's ear again.

"Shit!" the guard screams. "Not again!"

"No, Ananus, you can still arrest me. I don't mind, really," you calmly reply. "And this one's on the house, my son."

You touch the guard's ear and heal it again.

Ananus immediately slashes that ear off, too.

"Stop all of this healing nonsense! Nobody's buying your nice, innocent guy routine, Jesus. We didn't just fork over thirty big silver ones just to have you blink your baby blues and sway our hearts with all your magic tricks!"

"Ow," the guard moans. "Now I've only got one good ear and three useless ones! Woe is me!"

"Can it, you idiot!" Ananus screams. "You guards have great health insurance coverage. All you people do is lose limbs and then live off the Roman government for the rest of your miserable lives!"

You could spend all night regenerating this man's ear, but it's proving to be fairly pointless for all involved. It was sweet of Thomas to chop off another man's sensory organ for you, but you're totally resigned to let these people put you to death if that's what needs to happen.

You stoically plead with Ananus to set your disciples free, that you're the one who's guilty of being the Messiah.

In the middle of your speech, you hear the priests, guards, and other marauding townsfolk burst into laughter.

You turn to see what they're laughing at—your disciples have already turned tail and abandoned you.

Fantastic.

So the mob roughs you up a little, marches you into town, and brings you before a group of other important priests, scribes, and elders.

Secretly, Simon Peter follows the procession and hides amongst the multitude gathered in the courtroom.

The priests question you for a while, grilling you about all the miracles you've performed and about the radical doctrines you've been preaching. In a sad way, it's fun to relive some of these memories.

You can't help but feel a twinge of pride for all you've managed to accomplish within the past few months.

"What say you to the charges that you are the Christ the Messiah, the living son of our one true God?" one of the high priests screams.

"Duh," you answer. "I've only said that, like, ten thousand times in a thousand different towns."

"Guilty!" an elder screams.

"Blasphemy!" another elder cries.

Meanwhile, in the crowd, a servant leans over to Simon Peter and whispers, "That Jesus guy's a real wise-ass. You know him?"

"Who? Him?" Simon Peter says incredulously. "No way! I just love coming here in the middle of the night to watch blasphemers get their come-uppance. It's so refreshing."

"I'll shit to that, my friend," the servant laughs, squatting and taking a dump right on the court's floor.

Fucking classless servants…no wonder people are always making them clean things.

"The penalty for blasphemy, any blasphemy of any sort, is of course instant death!" the highest priest says, which brings a cheer from the crowd. "But I can't sentence you to death. Only the Governor can do that. Take this blasphemous pig-person before Pontious Pilate!"

The crowd goes nuts, the royal trumpeters start trumpeting, and the guards advance on you, slapping you around and pushing you out of the room.

Turn to PAGE 74

Heaven it is.

"Everybody stand back!"

You close your eyes, lift your hands, and pray for a miracle.

THWACK-BOOM!

Thunder cracks and clouds start swirling around in the sky.

Moments later, a monstrous pair of perfectly-shaped female breasts (complete with rosy, pert nipples) breaks through the clouds and hangs there naked for all of Creation to see.

Women scream and cover their children's eyes.

Every man and pubescent boy for miles around is instantly rendered retarded, their faces transfixed to the glistening globes above their heads.

"Oh Mommy…" Philip whimpers.

"Eh, it's just a couple of tits. Whoopty fucking shit," Thaddeus sniffs.

"Whaddya think, guys? That's a pretty good sign, eh?" you ask, all cocky-like.

"So what? We live in an unbelievably sexually repressed culture," Ananus snivels. "It'll take more than a pair of gorgeous woman's knockers to prove your divinity to us, Jesus."

"Yes, I should like to see what she's working with in the backside department, at the very least," another elder says, licking his lips.

You snap your fingers and the mammoth breasts disappear.

A glorious set of smooth feminine ass cheeks immediately pops out from behind the clouds in their place.

"Oy…that is some fantastic-looking tushie up there," one Pharisee drools.

"That's the most womanly nakedness I've ever witnessed," Ananus says, mesmerized. "And my wife's already borne me eight children!"

You clap your hands and the heavenly vision disappears.

"That's enough Heavenly signs and wonders for now," you say. "But there's lots more where that came from, you poor bunch of under-sexed perverts."

"You've got the goods, Jesus," a high priest snaps, poking a finger into your chest. "Even the eunuchs are all hot and horny now…and they don't have penises anymore."

"But that just means you fell right into our trap!" Ananus says. "Me and the Pharisees, we're officially *on to you!*"

"Yeah, you're on our shit list, pal! Right at the tippy-top," another priest cries.

"You guys did notice that I can summon female genitalia out of the freaking sky, right?" you reply. "The same plasma or whatever that flows through God's veins, assuming that He has veins, flows through mine! I'm hot shit. Hotter than a chipotle chili pepper stuffed with molten lava and whiskey diarrhea."

You slap an old woman so hard, that she spits out a few teeth. You cover her mouth with your hand, then quickly lower it, revealing a mouthful of shiny new teeth.

You're on fire and pissed off and everyone is scared shitless of you right now.

"I'm just getting started here, folks!" you scream. "So put me at the top of any list you want. Speaking of tops, I'm getting the urge to hike up to the top of that big-ass mountain over there. You can follow me and peek up my skirt at my righteous ballsack the whole way up for all I care. Peace out, bitches."

Your disciples have to sprint to keep up with you, leaving the Pharisees and other priests scratching their heads about you once again.

Turn to PAGE 65

130

You hack and slash your way through whatever this big place is—the bad guys' headquarters fortress—yeah, that's where you are, and you have to fight an endless amount of wimpy cronies and a few mini-bosses.

There are a few mind-bending puzzles to solve and some items that you need to collect and subsequently use to gain access to other parts of the headquarters, but at last, you make it past all of the challenges without losing too much of your energy and arrive at the doors of Pilate's chamber.

The last level. Finally.

You tighten your grip on the two heavy-duty sabers you just pulled out of a treasure chest behind a secret wall. You've upgraded them with as many power-up jewels as you could find and you've got a full health meter.

Time for the final showdown.

You kick open the doors and Pilate stands waiting for you all alone in the middle of the huge empty room, his arm muscles all oiled up and bulging from beneath his clothes. Normally, he wears a sensible judge's toga, but right now he's wearing a slick, futuristic neon-green ninja suit.

Pulling an ornate axe and a wicked-looking sword from their holsters on his back, he flashes you the most devilish of grins.

"I was expecting you for quite some time, Jesus," he hisses. "Let's play."

You charge across the room at each other, jumping at the last possible second, and tangling up in a fantastic, frenzied mid-air blade fight. Sparks fly and every strike is met with a perfect parry or block until Pilate slips up by a split second, leaving himself exposed just long enough for you to slice his abdomen wide open.

He drops his weapons and kneels before you as his guts start spilling out onto the floor. You stand over him, place your blades on either side of his neck, and stare into his eyes.

"Any last words, maggot?" you snarl.

"Yeah, just this one," he says with a laugh. "I'm not who you think I am, you fool!"

He reaches up and peels his face off. As soon as you see the first flash of bright red skin underneath his falsified face, you know whom you've really been dealing with.

It's Satan!

"Surprise surprise, Christey-kins," Satan mutters. "Go ahead. Finish off the job."

"You don't have to tempt me twice," you reply and lop his head off with one quick swipe of your bloody saber.

POOF!

Satan's body disappears in a wisp of acrid smoke.

Seconds later, the ground shakes and Satan's maniacal laughter echoes across the entire planet.

"Now you've done it, you idiot," God's voice rumbles down from Heaven. "You killed Satan before you could kill yourself on the cross! You've just damned every soul on Earth to an eternity in Hell. I forgot to tell you I had set up that deal with him a long time ago."

Oh shit, you think.

"Shit!" God adds.

Satan was the Anti-Christ all along! And by killing him, you just caused the anti-salvation of every human being's immortal soul!

Years later, after you drink yourself to death on cheap wine, you ascend to Heaven and find it absolutely deserted – just you, God, and a host of listless angels.

"My beautiful people…they're all stuck in Hell!" God cries.

You totally blew it and you feel awful.

And there's nothing you can do now except regret everything you ever did during your waste of an earthly life for the rest of eternal infinity…

THE END

132

You spot a tree hanging low over Lazarus' tomb.

Perfect...

Slipping your arms around the shoulders of Mary and Martha, you escort them a short distance away.

"Ladies, I'm going to raise your brother from the dead, by golly, but first I'm gonna need a little privacy," you tell them comfortingly. "So you two should just head into town and buy a couple of pretty new mourning sackcloths and some piles of ashes to throw all over yourselves. And I'll see you back here in about an hour."

"Anything you say, Jesus. And we'll be sure to gather some more weepers to help with all the extra weeping we'll need to do, too," Mary says.

The two women thank you and shuffle off toward town.

The second that you see Lazarus' sisters round the corner, you whisper to your disciples, "All right, boys, huddle up. We don't have much time. Andrew, you and Thaddeus open up that tomb and pull Lazarus' body out."

"Hmmm...handling a man's stiffened body...I'm all over it, JC!" Thaddeus giggles.

"James and James," you continue. "I need both of you tubby boys to go rustle up a mountain lion and hold him in that bush over there."

The Jameses hesitantly look at each other and gulp loudly.

"And Simon Peter, you go find me a helluva lot of rope," you say. "The rest of you, follow me over to this tree. We've got some work to do..."

An hour later, the women return from town to the sight of you sitting in a proud pose on a large rock.

"Welcome back, ladies," you grin. "The show, er, resurrection is about to begin. Have a seat."

They sit and you dramatically address them as if they were an audience of a thousand.

"What you are about to see...is real," you start in a mystical tone of voice. "As you can clearly see, I have nothing up my sleeves, there are no wires or switches...just the infinite holy power of the Almighty Lord our God. Come, join me in this most awesome and unbelievable journey of faith. I present to you, the Amazing Resurrection of The Once-Dead Lazarus."

With a flourish of your arms, you take a deep bow and wait for applause from Mary and Martha. When their polite cheering dies down, you stand and face the tomb.

"Lazarus...come forth!" you loudly demand.

The massive stone in front of the tomb slowly rolls to the side. Seconds later, the decomposing body of Lazarus, still in its burial rags, comes stumbling out with a groan.

"URRRHHHHH!!!"

You look up in the tree and wink at Simon Peter and Judas, who masterfully puppeteer Lazarus' corpse around with a series of tiny ropes.

The women gasp and clap in delight at the sight of their newly-risen loved one.

Behind your back, you flash a secret hand signal to the Jameses.

Suddenly, a ravenous mountain lion springs from a nearby bush and roars at Lazarus!

"Oh no!" you groan. "What an awful time for a mountain lion to attack!"

The women scream as Lazarus' body dances over to the lion.

"Heavens n' Betsy! Lazarus is protecting us from that mean old lion that randomly showed up!" you scream.

The lion pounces, tearing Lazarus' flailing corpse to bloody shreds.

You cue the other disciples and they pop up from behind another bush, in unison, and begin yelling and throwing stones at the mountain lion until it scampers off.

You sadly turn back to the women, who have started up with all their goddamned wailing again.

"I'm sorry, Mary and Martha, but I can't resurrect someone twice. Not to mention, there's not much left for me to work with," you say, gesturing to the gory pile of bones on the ground.

"It's ok, Jesus," Mary says. "You did your best and that's all that matters."

"Ladies, it's been our pleasure," Bart says. "We shall now be on our merry way."

You and the disciples line up in a row, take a nice bow, and turn to leave.

As you speed away from the tomb, you whisper to your disciples that you can't believe your improvised resurrection ruse worked.

"I don't believe it, either, even though I saw it happen with my own two eyes," agrees Thomas.

"Let's just hope that my readers can believe it!" Matthew says.

You share a hearty laugh at that and head off into the setting sun.

Turn to PAGE 112

134

You enjoy a leisurely stroll around Heaven for a few minutes, soaking up all the otherworldly sights and smells.

There's a lot of fun trouble to get into up here, you think.

You begin flirting with a sexy, big-breasted archangel near the Pearly Gates, and just when you're about to seal the deal for real, a messenger angel tugs on your robe sleeve and informs you that it's already been two Earth days since you left.

You forgot that Heaven runs on God's time, which is much faster than Earth's time! Dammit!

You've got to keep your promise that you'll arise from the dead in three days, so you dive off the heavenly cloud you're standing on and float back down to Earth.

Wheeee! It's fun being a spirit. You should die more often.

You fly back up to Heaven. Then you slowly drop to Earth again.

You repeat this process for quite some time.

Eventually, you arrive at your tomb. It's a spacious place, and not nearly as dank as you had imagined.

You float over to your corpse, which lies on a long stone shelf, wrapped up in a shroud.

Ewww, it's all wormy and smelly. Hmmm…maybe you should find a different body to inhabit. It is your big comeback special and you can't look all sickly and bloated and, well, recently tortured to death.

Your Old Man just said you had to check up on your disciples. He didn't specify that you had to actually do it *in your old body*. But you can't appear to them in your current glowing, indeterminate spiritual form, either. You'd blow their feeble minds if you did that.

Surely there's got to be a fresher, less manhandled corpse lying around here somewhere.

However, it might also prove unwise to make any brash decisions from here on out. You've come so close to being finished with this earthly mission and it would be a real shame to screw up now.

Yes, just as the prologue of this book prophesied pages upon pages ago, even in death, there are still choices to be made…

If you look for a better body, turn to PAGE 136

If you get back in your own body, turn to PAGE 151

You don't think you're ready to make a deal with the devil, but you figure that this is all probably a hallucination anyway and you could use a little entertainment before you die in the middle of nowhere, so you tell Satan to continue playing his little game.

"Terrific!" he says, overjoyed. "So here's how it works. You like choosing things, don't you? *Of course* you do! So I've created a little game of choice-choosing. A tempting of your will, if you will. I'll present you with three choices and you just have to pick one. Sound easy enough?"

"Yeah, whatever," you reply.

"Your first choice is to turn these stones to bread and eat them."

He points at some rocks that you actually thought were loaves of bread earlier, since your starving brain has been morphing things that you see into different foods. You lick one to make sure it's really just a rock. Yep. Limestone with a granite aftertaste.

"I have to choke down all this bread? Without any water?"

"Shut up!" Satan screams. "This is my game. I'm the tempter, you're the temptee. I tempt, you lie there and make bad decisions! Ok?"

You shrug your bony shoulders.

"Now, your second choice is to jump off that cliff right there and call down a bunch of angels to come save you from splattering all over the ground below," Satan says proudly.

"And just what good would that do me?" you ask.

"I'm not sure," Satan says, scratching his head. "It'll look cool."

"Yeah, but it doesn't put food in my belly or help get me out of this blasted wilderness," you retort. "Plus, I'm scared of heights. Honestly, that one's not all that tempting to me."

"Okay, damn you! Forget that choice," Satan snaps. "Your other choice is to bow down and worship me. And if you do that, I'll make you the king of the world. Cool, huh? Eat some bread or rule the whole world, take your pick."

He's not very good at this, you think as you ponder your options.

If you turn stones to bread, turn to PAGE 64

If you worship Satan, turn to PAGE 83

If you cheat and choose neither of Satan's options, turn to PAGE 154

136

Your pride trumps your humility and you float out of the tomb to search for an alternate body to cavort around in.

Soon enough, you stumble upon a tree with a man's body dangling from its neck on a rope in one of its branches.

When the corpse spins toward you, you see that it's Judas! Looks like the sucker did himself in just a few minutes ago. A bag of silver lies spilled out under his feet. The guilt of his betrayal must've been too much for him.

"All the money in the world just wasn't enough for you, was it?" you ask his limp carcass. "Well, I'm not only a big fan of irony and just deserts, but I also doubt I could find a fresher body than this!"

You cut his body down and jump into it. Not bad. A little stiff, but good muscle tone. Judas took care of himself, the old rascal. You scoop up all the silver and start off toward the nearest town.

When you finally track your disciples down, things don't go exactly as you planned. Because you look and sound just like the traitorous Judas, they refuse to speak to you. After Thomas swipes at your ear with a sword, you decide that maybe showing up as Judas wasn't the best idea and you make a hasty retreat.

You stash Judas' body and ascend back up to Heaven, but when you get there, God informs you that since you've royally screwed everything up, He's making you a mortal again. He flicks you back into the body of Judas on Earth and now you're really stuck.

Since you (Jesus Christ) never returned to inspire and spur on your disciples, they eventually start following some other guy who claims that he's the real Son of God. Of course, he ends up being just another self-delusional douchebag, but they remain faithful until the bitter end, just as they did with you.

With nothing better to do on this miserable planet, you set out to indulge in some of your darkest fantasies – you hunt down that murderous bastard Barabbas and give him the proper crucifixion he deserved, you sweep Mary Magdalene off her feet and make her your wife, and you even build a replica of Noah's Ark and sail it around the world.

You live a long and fulfilling life. But every once in a while, when it's quiet and you're all alone, you think about how much fun it was in your first earthly life, when you were mankind's only hope for a savior.

At times like this, you get that itch, the one that makes you want to start preaching and healing again…

THE END

What the hell? A little charity and trust never hurt nobody, you think.
"Okay, Judas…you're in," you tell him. "You're an apostle."
"You haven't seen the last of me, Jesus!" Judas screams.
You look at him quizzically.
"Oh. Um. Never mind. Heh heh…You made the right choice," he says. Then he kisses you on the cheek and disappears into the small crowd of your followers.

So you and your twelve new friends sort of wander the dusty, sun-scorched countryside for a few weeks, living off the land, sharing your bizarre philosophies about what's wrong with the world today, and meeting lots of diseased and destitute people (who also seem to flock to you everywhere you go for some reason).

Sometimes you get inspired and spout a little wisdom here and there.

For some reason, the crowds always seem to eat it up.

You lay your hands on some of the sick people that you meet, wishing them well, and pretty soon, rumors start spreading that you've got a healing touch.

You feel like a twentieth century politician on the campaign trail, even though you don't know what that exactly means yet.

It's a nice feeling, though.

One day, as you sit enjoying the shade of a particularly nice birch tree, Bartholomew appears at your side.

"Jesus. Baby," he begins. "I love what you're doing, but so far it's all been very disorganized and random. You've been hanging around here like a pillar of salt for three days. We need to get something solid going."

"Aw, but we're having such a groovy time, Bart," you reply.

"I know, JC, but there are hundreds upon hundreds of people scrambling around for tickets to hear you speak. I don't know who this John the Baptist fellow is, but he's been preaching you up around town, too. Guy had impressive PR skills."

"Wait…what do you mean 'had?'" you ask.

"You didn't hear? John got his head chopped off and served up on a silver platter by King Herod last night."

You are utterly shocked to hear this. You didn't know that they made silver platters big enough to hold a human head. You also wonder what someone does with the head once it's been served to them in such a manner.

Turn to the NEXT PAGE

138

"Yo! JC! Listen to me, baby. Focus," Bart continues. "You're special. I don't know who or what you are, exactly. Some call you the second coming of the prophet Joshua, others the heir to jolly old King David. I've even heard a few people say you're gonna be the next freaking Moses."

Whoa. Now that's a sobering thought.

"I say let 'em think what they want," Bart says, slapping you on the back. "All I know is that everybody's sick and unhappy and they need a savior. That's you, babe! You're the Messiah! And the world needs you!"

He's right. As much as you've been denying this to yourself for the past few weeks, God must have sent you here for a reason. And a damn good one, at that!

You're going to be the divine savior of all mankind!

"You sure do talk fast and pretty, Bart," you say. "What did you do for a living before you joined up with me and all these other goofballs?"

"I was a wood-bringer," he replies.

"What does a wood-bringer do?"

"Basically…if somebody needed wood, I brought it to them."

"That's a real job?"

"Not really, but neither is being the Messiah, but you seem to be doing all right with that."

He raises a good point.

"So now that we're on the same page," Bart continues. "I've been talking with Judas and the guys and we all agree that we're pretty tired of living like a bunch of hungry, homeless, penniless bums. We need some organization, a purpose to our wandering. Or at the very least, we should give the illusion that we have an agenda."

"I'm following you," you say, deep in thought.

"No. *We* are following *you*. Don't you ever forget that," he says, staring into your eyes. "And as your loyal followers, we're saying that it's time to follow you to the next level."

Judas pops up out of nowhere and continues, "And where is that next level, you ask? Sainthood? Ha! Leave that stuff to the peace-loving pussies of the world! Prophet? Please! In their dreams! King of Kings and Lord of Lords? Whoa. Now we're talking!"

Your head is spinning, trying to absorb all of this.

Bart slips his arm around your shoulders and hugs you tightly.

"Judas here has some beautiful ideas about where we could take this Son of God ministry thing—shelves crammed with books about your life written by men of dubious characters, oversized mega-churches based on your teachings, bookmarks with out-of-context quotes from you printed on them to stick inside the books—the possibilities are endless!"

"How about this, Jesus?" Judas asks, squeezing your other arm hard enough to make you wince. "Have you ever had your own holiday?"

"No, I can't say that I have," you say, confused and starting to lose some feeling in your upper body from all the squeezing.

"How would you like to have two? You listen to us, start acting like the one true flesh and blood incarnation of the Almighty Jehovah, and we'll have the whole world taking a day off work and school just to sit around and celebrate the day you were born *and* the day that you died."

They stop talking and anxiously look at you.

"Gee, I don't know what to say, guys. Sounds like you've pulled together a real foolproof, win-win kind of plan here. I'm in!"

"Hey, it's God's plan, not ours," Judas says. "Remember that, especially if people ask you about it."

The two men whoop with delight, high-five each other, and tickle you mercilessly in a flurry of excited hugs.

"This is great news, baby!" Bart says. "Let's hit the sand running! Right now I've got you booked for an appearance at a wedding party, a brief sermon and boat ride to Nazareth, where I think you'll be huge—the whole local boy makes good story—and a lengthier sermon on that mount over there. You can do one or you can do all three, but you've got to choose which one to do first. Lord knows you can't be everywhere at once! Or maybe you can, I don't know. I mean, omnipotence has to have its limits, right?"

It looks like you have another big decision to make.

If you attend the wedding, turn to PAGE 4

If you preach the sermon on the mount, turn to PAGE 92

If you ride the boat to Nazareth, turn to PAGE 157

140

"WHAT THE FUCK DID YOU DO TO ME?" the man screams.

Although really, he can't technically be classified as a man now, seeing as how you just turned his maimed penis into a shiny new vagina.

Satan rolls around on the ground in glee.

"I-I-I'm truly sorry," you say to the transsexual thing freaking out in front of you. "I don't know what happened. I'm still trying to fully understand how my powers work. Look on the bright side, though. You might have lady parts now instead of man parts, but at least they're clean, healthy lady parts."

"I don't want to have a woman's vagina between my thighs!" the man cries. "What will my wives say when it's time for me to have bland, orthodox sex with them? I'm too ashamed to go on living like this!"

He hikes up the hem of his robe and runs off into the wilderness, never to be seen again.

"Nice to know I can always cunt, I mean count, on you for a good laugh, Jesus!" Satan roars between bouts of laughter. "Some savior you turned out to be!"

"Don't listen to him, Jesus," John says. "You're a fine Messiah. I mean, nobody's perfect, even you. But don't worry, I'm going to say that you were immaculate and blameless in the book that I'm writing."

"Yeah, me and all the other guys will be sure to lie about all your screw-ups in our books, too," Matthew reassures you.

"Looks like Daddy up in Heaven sent the wrong little boy to do a man's job," Satan smirks.

You've just accidentally performed the world's first sex change operation on that poor guy. You feel terrible.

"Face it, Jesus," Satan continues. "You're a shitty Messiah. Why don't you go home and whittle some wood with your earthly father where you belong?"

You try to hide the fact that his harsh words are starting to sting a little.

What makes it worse is that some poor she-male's blood could be on your hands if he/she decides to do something stupid like taking his/her own life.

Maybe Satan is right for once…you have no business trying to be the Messiah.

"Don't feel *that* bad, Jesus," James #2 says. "I mean, seeing you zap a vagina onto that guy was pretty funny, right? At least the first few seconds were, but then it kinda turned into a real bummer."

"I gotta admit that I think he was cute, then not cute, then kind of cute again," Thaddeus says. "Point being that I'd probably fuck him."

None of this is making you feel any better about what just happened.

Bart grabs you by the shoulders and looks you square in the eye.

"Jesus, I say you forget that she-he and forget whatever this Satan guy is telling you. You've got lots more preaching and loving to give this world. Let's continue to Jericho and move onward and upward."

"Hey, what's the opposite of a chick with a dick?" Satan asks. "Cuz that's what that poor bastard with the vagina is right now."

Man, Satan really knows how to get under your skin...

Tad gently taps you on the shoulder and interrupts your thoughts.

"Hey, you think you could hook me up with an extra butthole? Is that too much to ask? Are you willing to perform cosmetic, non-life-threatening kinds of miracles like that?"

You stare at him blankly.

Jesus Christ, who are these people and what are you doing with your life?

Should you allow your insecurities to overwhelm you or should you rebuke Satan once again and stubbornly push ahead in your quest?

If you wimp out and take Satan's criticisms to heart, turn to PAGE 82

If you stand up for yourself, disregard Satan, and head to Jericho, turn to the NEXT PAGE

142

It's a lengthy, event-free journey to Jericho, and when you arrive, you immediately run through your whole Messiah schtick – spouting drawn-out sermons and parables, healing sick people, and having strange women come wash your feet while weeping and praising you.

One day as you're strolling through town, a man dressed up in all the fancy garb of a high priest jumps out from around a corner and sticks a bony finger into your chest. A bunch of other similarly-dressed guys follow at his heel.

"Hey! You're that Jesus fella!" he shouts. "We've seen your tax records this year. They're atrocious! Why haven't you paid them yet?"

You look at him, baffled.

"Whoa. Back off from the alleged Chosen One, buster," Thomas says, getting in the man's face. "Or else I'll pull your kidneys out through your belly button."

It's really nice having a homicidal maniac for a friend.

Recognition dawns on Matthew's face.

"Say, you're Ananus, aren't you?"

"Yes, I'm Ananus," the priest replies. "What of it?"

"Yeah, more like an anus hole, if you ask me!" you snort.

"No, you're an anus, Jesus!" Ananus says bitterly. "I'm Ananus."

You roll your eyes.

"Pffft! Whatever. Your anus can go to Uranus for all I care, anus."

"Right after you kiss my anus, you dumb-anus," Ananus grumbles.

"Stop it you two!" Matthew says. "For real Jesus, this guy really is Ananus."

"Yeah, I can see that, Matthew!" you scream.

"Hey, I don't mean to 'butt' in on the convo here," Tad says. "But whose anus are we talking about and can I get in on some of that action?"

"Everybody shoosh up," Bart says. "Jesus, what Matthew is trying to tell you is that this guy's name is 'Ananus.' He's a high priest of the Pharisees, the religious authorities who feel threatened by you. That's who all these other guys are."

"Oh!" you say, slapping your forehead. "I gotcha. But for the record, I still think Ananus is an anus."

"Whatever. Now let me handle this tax issue," Judas says, dumping some coins out of his coin pouch.

The priests glance at the coins.

"Nope! That's not enough," Ananus says. "He owes more than that."

Judas drops the entire pouch at his feet.

"Ha! You're gonna need six whole pouches' worth of coins to cover his tax debts," another priest says smugly.

Judas shrugs and looks at you worriedly. That's all he's got.

"What…can't you guys cut me a break just this once? I'm doing God's work over here!" you plead with the priests. "Why can't we discuss this later? Or, like, not at all, ever?"

The Pharisees think for a second, puzzled.

"Because we're the Pharisees and we don't like you Messiah-types. You give our religion a bad name," Ananus says. "You, that loony John the Baptist, that other guy Honi who sat in a circle for six months and prayed for rain, and what's-his-name the Egyptian dude who tried to destroy the walls of Jerusalem by marching around them for weeks. I mean, you're a nice guy and all, Jesus, but you've got a real Son-of-God complex, you know?"

"Plus, attendance and revenue is dropping in their temple services," Matthew whispers in your ear. "They blame you, of course."

You notice that now a crowd has gathered and people are starting to murmur doubtful things about you.

Maybe the priests are right. You've become too much of a radical sensation. Maybe the people just need another mild-mannered local prophet, not some world-traveling, miracle-working Messiah superstar…

"Whatever. This is stupid," you say. "I don't have to justify my actions to you people. I'm the everlasting Son of God. I had to learn to live with it and so do you!"

This last statement produces some gasps from the crowd.

"See what I mean?" Ananus screams to the crowd. "He's crazy!"

Bart jumps in front of you in an attempt to regain some control of the situation.

"What Jesus means to say is that he's really tired and needs a little break. We'll prepare a public statement later and hold a press conference where you can ask him further questions regarding the matter."

As you wonder aloud what a press conference is, Bart turns to you and whispers, "Ix-nay on the un-say of odd-gay alk-tay."

"What's that about an odd gay?" Tad chirps.

Before you can answer, you hear a rustle in the tree above you.

"Psst! Hey Jesus!"

You look up and see a weird little man sitting on one of the lower branches, smiling at you.

Turn to the NEXT PAGE

144

"Hey! Come over to my house, dude," the man calls down in a hushed voice. "I can easily get you out of your tax debacle if you do!"

"Um, who are you and why are you hiding in that tree?" you ask.

"We can totally see and hear everything that you two are talking about," Ananus says. "So you can stop whispering."

"Really? Shit!" the guy says. "Well, the name's Zaccheus. Come to my house and do me one little favor and I'll do you an even bigger one."

James #2 grabs your arm.

"These Pharisee people mean business. We can't just ignore them."

"They have the power of the Roman government behind them," James #1 adds.

"Can't I just, like, hold up some money and make it multiply like I did with that fish and bread a while back?" you ask.

"Yeah, I doubt the banks probably would appreciate that sort of behavior. We don't need anymore enemies," Bart says. "I think you should just walk away, take a breather, and think of another way out of this situation."

You look over and see Judas whispering with a group of priests. He's probably trying to cut some kind of an under-the-table deal to get them off your back.

What a good guy that Judas is...

It doesn't look like you're going to be able to bullshit your way out of this mess, so your only options are to either take a break and figure out how you're going to evade this tax evasion or to follow this weird tree-climbing stranger, Zaccheus, to his house.

Seems like a no-brainer, right?

If you go along with Zaccheus, turn to PAGE 10

If you take a break and think, turn to PAGE 121

An indeterminate number of hours pass.

During this time, you experience many wonderful hallucinations, some of which include:

You discovering that your belly button is actually just the entrance to a nest filled with millions of friendly ants;

Simon Peter designing an odd-looking contraption with rotating blades that he claims will one day allow human beings to fly;

And John bravely diving into the sand and engaging in hand-to-hand combat with a bunch of gigantic snail-like creatures who were apparently invading Earth from the moon.

When the mushrooms finally wear off and you fade back into consciousness, you find yourself sitting in a small semi-circle with James #2, John, and Simon Peter.

"For God so loved the world," John says. "That He gave His only begotten son, that whosoever believeth in him, should not perish, but have everlasting life."

"Ooh, good one, John!" Simon Peter says.

"I kind of cheated on that one," John replies. "That's a passage from my book—Chapter 3, verse 16."

You groan, clutching at your aching head and burning stomach.

"Hey! Welcome back to reality, Jesus," James #2 says, patting your leg. "We're playing the 'For God So Loved the World Game.' It's your turn."

God…gave His son…

That reminds you—you now have the delightful pleasure of laying down your life like a sacrificial lamb for all of humanity's sins at some point in the near future.

Blorg.

"Guys, I'm really not in the mood to talk about God and love and goodwill and all that nonsense right now," you grumble.

"Aw, come, Jesus," John whines. "Humor us just this once. We promise we won't bug you about anything else for a while."

Turn to the NEXT PAGE

146

"All right," you say, caving in. "I can't stay mad at those chubby cheeks of yours, John."

John giggles and blushes. You clear your throat and focus.

"Here goes…For God so loved the shitty, retarded world, that He forced His only son, who's probably the nicest guy to ever roam this turdball of a world, to effectively commit suicide, all so that His stupid human creations can keep fucking up and ignoring their responsibilities time and time again, and when they die, they'll still get to spend eternity in Paradise, which will be pretty goddamn awkward for God's son Jesus, who will also have to share Paradise with all these self-absorbed assholes forever and ever. How's that?"

The three men look at you in stunned silence.

"Um, I think I prefer John's version," Simon Peter finally says. "Maybe it's time to head back down to the rest of the disciples. It'll give you some time to cool off, big guy."

The four of you start descending the mountain.

"I have to remember those 'shrooms for when I write my next book, Revelations," John says. "It's going to be this sort of post-apocalyptic, sci-fi thriller about the ultimate showdown between good and evil and I'll need some good inspiration for the really crazy parts."

You remain silent for the rest of the mount-descending, completely lost in dark thoughts.

When you get to the bottom and wake up your other disciples, Bartholomew freaks out and says that you've gotten way behind on the day's schedule, so now you've got to choose between blessing a bunch of schoolchildren or saying "woe" to a bunch of whoremongers.

You're still feeling out of sorts and you aren't sure whether you belong around children or loose women right now, but you've got to pick *something* for crying out loud…

If you head to the whorehouse, turn to PAGE 97

If you head to the school, turn to PAGE 100

Prophecy schmophecy. You're going to do this thing on your terms.

"No more fancy theatrics," you say, pushing past your disciples and walking into the city on your own two blessed feet.

Since it's the middle of the day, the marketplace is a busy, crowded place and nobody's paying much attention to you.

Shit! You can't compete with all this noisy commerce!

You walk over and order the gatekeepers to close the city gates so nobody can come in or out. For some reason, they do as they're told, which is both unexpected and awesome.

Finally, some respect up in this mug!

"Attention all townspeople!" you call out to the bustling marketplace. "I am Jesus Christ of Nazareth, the Son of God, and this is my house! I've come to save your eternal souls from damnation and absolve you from your disgusting, sinful habits. Also, I love you very much."

For a second, everyone is quiet. Then they turn right back to their business at hand, as if you never existed.

This, of course, greatly upsets you. So much so, that you start throwing a tantrum and accidentally kick a lamp over onto a large, extremely dry haystack.

Seconds later, a towering inferno is raging across the market! Everyone panics and starts trampling each other. They can't get the gates open fast enough and the whole city of Jerusalem burns to the ground within the hour.

Burnt to a crisp like everyone else, your spirit floats up to Heaven.

"For shame. I'm afraid the burning's just begun for you, young man," God says disapprovingly.

As punishment for failing to save mankind, God grounds you, sending you down to Hell for a few thousand years to think about what you did.

By the time you're finally able to see Earth again, the humans have long since extinguished themselves due to war, famine, and blatantly raping the planet's ecosystem.

So much for that!

THE END

148

"I do have a good reason not to be executed, your honor, sir, Mr. Governor. I learned a valuable lesson today. I learned that although I may not like what I've been prophesied to do with my life, it doesn't matter. As the one and only Son of God, if I don't let you all kill me today, well, who the hell else is going to sacrifice themselves for everybody's sake?"

All is quiet in the great hall for a moment.

"Uh, and children, you need to stay in school and keep off drugs until you're all grown up into responsible, consenting adults," you add.

Pilate clears his throat. "You have thoroughly swayed the heart of this court, Jesus. I hereby repeal your sentence!"

You breathe a sigh of relief. "So I'm free to go?"

"Oh no," Pilate replies with a laugh. "No no no no no no, silly man. You're still sentenced to die, blasphemer. But we'll make it much easier on you with our gentlest, most merciful death…a Comfy-Fixion!"

With that, the guards patiently guide you into an outside courtyard, politely ask you to change out of your robe and into a modest, yet mildly embarrassing silk pantsuit, and proceed to make bothersome inquiries into your personal life and force you to listen to them sing annoying songs in loud voices for several hours.

After that, they carefully bend you over a padded rock and lay a series of irritating fabrics across the flesh of your back. Next, you must endure a terrible beard-trimming from a blind guy using a pair of slightly dulled clippers. A few guards restrain you while another guard tickles you relentlessly all over your body with an ostrich feather. At one point, you are gingerly pelted with thousands upon thousands of marshmallows.

Finally, some guards lay you upon a very comfortable contraption that looks like a soft, narrow bed with walls. One of the guards refers to it as a "couch" and you are encouraged to voluntarily strap yourself onto it. They hoist you and the couch up fifteen feet into the air on a long wooden pole and immediately start feeding you an endless diet of honey and fried lamb cracklin's.

It takes sixty-two days for you to die. You would've lasted a lot longer if not for that nasty infection you got after one of your many horrific full-body sunburns. At the time of your death, you had gained over eighty pounds, so eventually, you would've died from a heart attack.

For all Eternity, however, your believers will weep when they tell the story of how you died up on the couch for all of their sins. They will also enjoy their lengthy sixty-two-day Easter holidays.

THE END

150

You utter the quick, shrill whistle that signals to John that the ox dung has indeed hit the proverbial fanning slave. He tosses you his sword and you deftly slice off the guard's other ear.

It's on mother-fornicators!

"I'll do the same to any man who tries to arrest me!" you scream.

The guards rush forward and dog pile on top of you. You burst up from their midst, healing yourself and chopping off ear after ear. It's absolute mayhem and you're loving every second of it.

Your disciples attempt to join the fracas, but since they are a bunch of half-starved weaklings with no combat training, the guards effortlessly massacre all of them.

You accidentally break your blade on a nearby Prayer Rock, and the mob of guards, angry and mostly earless now, manage to bind your arms behind you.

Perhaps you should have done more than just hack off their ears!

They cart you off into the city and stand you before the high priest.

"So this is the mighty Jesus," the high priest sniffs.

"If thou hath ears to hear, thou better recognize, bitch," you retort.

"Uh huh," he replies. "I've heard enough. Send him to the Governor, Pontious Pilate!"

"How 'bout I send yer ass to Pilate on a silver platter, bub?" you growl, effortlessly snapping the bindings off your arms.

"Guards! I want this foul-mouthed jackanape's head on a platter NOW!" the priest screams. "Someone else get a head-carrying platter!"

In one swift motion, you yank a spear out of a nearby guard's hands and make a shish kebab out of the six guards behind you.

It's on again, whoremongers!

Wave after wave of guards attack, but they're no match for your instant self-healing ability and pent-up, nerdy rage. Dozens of men die at your hands and their blood splatters up and down your perfect killing machine of a body from head-to-toe.

After a really cool, drawn-out swordfight between you and the captain of the guards, you calmly strut up to the high priest's throne thingy, where he cowers and whimpers like a baby. You grab him by the throat and bring his face up close to yours. You can smell that he's soiled himself out of sheer terror.

"Take me to Pilate, you Roman dog," you snarl.

Turn to PAGE 130

Things tend to get funky when you veer from the simple path that God preordained for you, so you'll stick to the script on this one and use your old body to do God's bidding.

Your spirit plops back into your smelly old corpse, and suddenly your body is almost as good as new!

Besides a couple of open wounds on your wrists and feet from the crucifixion nails, your body is fresher than it was before you died!

You gotta have faith, you think as you cast a tender smile Heavenward.

You find your disciples mourning in a nearby village, and after a short celebratory exchange, you inform them that you have to return to Heaven now and that it's their responsibility to carry out your legacy and message of hope and love for all mankind.

For once, they seem to understand what you're talking about and they present you with an exciting proposal of how they plan to spread your gospel. They show you an impressive array of publishing flowcharts, demographic maps, proposal drafts, merchandising prospectuses, and even a really neat architectural model of the first-ever Christian church.

Overall, it's a surprisingly solid, Earth-encompassing, millennia-spanning business plan.

Congratulations! You have successfully fulfilled your role as humanity's savior and you've inspired a huge religious movement!

After you've allowed Thomas to dig his fingers around in your wounds to convince him that you're really you and that you've risen from the grave like you said you would, you share some tearful goodbyes with your friends and ascend back to Heaven.

Meanwhile, lurking behind a nearby bushel and watching the entire scene, Satan rubs his hands together in a nefarious fashion.

"So…Jesus thinks he's redeemed mankind for all Eternity, does he?" Satan says aloud, addressing no one in particular. "Lucky for me, I've got my own Christ to send out into the world, only it's the exact opposite kind of Christ—The Anti-Christ, if you will! But I'll save his little, should I say, 'revelation' for later…Mwaa-hahahahaaaaaa!"

Satan mischievously tweaks his little mustache and dances around in glee.

This could mean loads of trouble for God's beloved humans in the future, but for now, everything seems to be groovy.

Well done, thou good and faithful servant.

And all of God's people said…Amen.

THE END

152

"Tarry here for just a moment," you say and excuse yourself from the room.

You rush over to the temple, approach Ananus, and ask him how much the priests paid Judas to betray you to them.

"Thirty pieces of silver," Ananus replies. "The standard fee for all suspected Messiah betrayals."

"Cool. I'll undercut him and do it for twenty-five silvers," you curtly say. "He's the one going around claiming to be God's divine son and all that jazz."

"I won't even bother asking you what the hell 'jazz' is," Ananus says warily. "Twenty-five silvers, you say? What a bargain!"

"Judas has done us no wrong," another priest says. "But we'd be fools to pass up a steal like this! You've got yourself a deal, Jesus!"

They hand over the dough, call some guards, and you lead everyone over to McDaniel's to deliver Judas, a relatively innocent man, into their hands.

Before you enter, you turn to the priests and say, "Remember, Judas will be the man that I kiss."

"We know what Judas looks like," Ananus says. "We've been secretly plotting your murder with him for months."

"Shut up and just let me do it my way, ok?" you snap.

You walk in and boldly kiss Judas, right on the mouth. He tastes like grape leaves and garlic.

"What is the meaning of this?" Judas asks. "*I'm* supposed to be the one kissing and consequently betraying *you*!"

The guards seize Judas and haul him away. Ananus and the other priests respectfully nod at you and exit.

"That was pretty slick of me, huh?" you ask, wiggling your eyebrows at your disciples, all of whom are too shocked to finish their slices of key lime pie at this point.

They shake their heads disappointedly.

"Come on…don't be like that, guys. If I didn't do it to him, he was going to do it to me!"

No one says a word.

Matthew pulls the latest revision of the scroll he was writing about you out of his beard and rips it in half.

"Aw, sheesh! Get over yourselves. Let's at least finish this lovely meal together like the good old days, and then I promise we'll talk about my betrayal of Judas," you suggest.

Again, no one speaks.

"Mmm…I could go for some fried bananas," you offer. "Who's with me?"

As your party finishes the Last Supper, all of your lame attempts at conversation are met with a depressing and absolute silence.

At the meal's conclusion, one-by-one, your disciples mutter different excuses about why they need to shuffle off and then they proceed to do so.

It slowly dawns on you that the magic of your ministry is gone and that you'll never see any of them again.

"Well, it sure was a hoot while it lasted," you tell John, the last of the disciples to go.

You go to pinch his chubby, oh-so-pinchable cheeks, but he shies away from your hand and slowly backs out of the restaurant and into the night.

You return home to Galilee and go back to work for your earthly father in his carpentry shop.

Two months later, a large cypress splinter in your arm gets a nasty infection and a doctor has to lop off the gangrenous limb before it kills you.

Unfortunately, he botches that procedure and you wind up bleeding to death on his surgical rock.

Looks like in the end you really wound up betraying yourself, didn't you, Jesus?

THE END

154

"You know, Satan, much to your dismay, I'm not going to play your little baby games anymore," you tell Satan, much to his dismay. "I can find my way out of this wilderness on my own. I can do all things through me who strengthens me."

"Awww, you can't do that! It's not fair," Satan exclaims, stomping his little goat feet in annoyance.

"Oh, go worship yourself," you respond, heaving a stone at Satan and striking him in the head.

"Oof! Them stones ain't soft like no bread!" Satan yelps, stumbling backwards and falling over the side of the cliff.

You don't hear a thud signaling his demise and you can't help but think that you haven't seen the last of that wily character…

Just then, a couple of angels swoop down from Heaven and give you a round of high-fives for overcoming Satan's temptations.

Where were these assholes five minutes ago when you needed them most?

Suddenly refreshed and filled with the indescribable power of absolute moral superiority, you dust your hands off and head down the mountain, whistling a happy tune and instinctively following the path out of the terrible wilderness and into Galilee.

Upon your entrance into one of Galilee's cities, you run into Simon Peter Timothy at a public water well.

He tells you that while you were wandering in the wilderness and discovering important things about yourself, he made a fortune performing live bird-themed comedy shows with your beloved pet dove Perchy.

Unfortunately, though, he spent most of that money on tasteless women and cheap saltwater taffy, which is Galilee's main export item.

You shake your head and are about to lecture your friend about his frivolous way of living life when Simon Peter Timothy grabs your arm and says he is about to use the last of his money to eat a seven-course dinner of wild rabbit cheese and camel hair tacos before he hops on a chariot to Galilee.

He insists that you join him.

Having just starved yourself for a few weeks, you can't argue with him about that.

Turn to PAGE 17

Judas runs off and returns a few minutes later, leading a camel that's only got three legs!

"Aw man! I don't wanna ride that thing. People will think I'm an asshole," you whine. "Is it too late for me to choose the donkey?"

"The ass is dead now," Judas says. "It was bred specifically to fulfill the Messianic prophecy, and when that fell through half an hour ago, they slaughtered it for dinner later."

You look at the pitiable creature. Simply standing up for an extended amount of time seems to be a difficult enough endeavor for it to handle.

"I'd rather just triumphantly walk into the city than ride that abomination anywhere."

"Suit yourself," Judas replies.

So you start walking toward the city's gates. On the way, you step into a shallow hole and fall, twisting your ankle something fierce in the process. You can't even stand on it now.

"Son of a bitch!" you cry out.

Now you have no choice. You'll have to ride the fucking tripod camel.

"Maybe you can just fulfill, like, half of the prophecy and that'll be good enough," Tad suggests. "Even a third of it would be nice."

So an hour later, you're slowly riding the three-legged camel into Jerusalem. It's not the best entrance, but it's not all that bad.

You even get some nods and waves from a few townspeople, but it's not like they're paving your path with palm branches or anything.

Right about that time, your camel starts bumping into people and stumbling all over the place.

Before you can dismount, it's crushed an entire fruit stand and trampled a small child to death.

When word gets around about your embarrassing fiasco of a ride into Jerusalem, everyone loses faith and interest in you.

Over the next few days, your healing powers fade away, and soon enough, you've become just another raving lunatic roaming the city walls, cutting yourself with sharp stones, and claiming to be the key to humanity's salvation...

THE END

156

"Give a man a fish and he'll eat today. Teach a man to fish and he'll eat for life," you say, feeling rather quote-worthy today.

You glance back at Matthew, and he's obediently nodding and writing all of your speech down.

"Matt, m'boy," you say, "Go ahead and tack this little gem onto the end of that sentence: 'Laugh like you're a baby, love like there's no tomorrow, and dance like nobody's watching.'"

You start to explain some basic agricultural techniques to the multitude. The James twins feel guilty and even donate some of their corn kernels to help get the crops started.

However, once the famished multitude realizes that it will require months of improbable, heavy rains and hard labor for just the chance of a decent harvest to arrive, they turn on you and tear you to pieces.

Whipped into a starved, cannibalistic rage, the crowd then feasts upon your entrails.

Miraculously, there is enough of your body to go around, as if the pieces of your flesh are multiplying!

By sundown, all four thousand people (including your disciples) are patting their full bellies, lazily joking around and telling stories.

Gnawing on one of your hundreds of rib bones, Matthew hastily rubs out your "teach a man to fish" quote from his record of your teachings.

"Maybe that would make for a good Chinese proverb instead," he says.

"Yeah," Bartholomew agrees. "Tomorrow we should head over to the Orient and start hanging around that Confucius guy."

No one argues with him about that.

THE END

Later, you're on a boat headed for Nazareth.

After delivering a short sermon to your eager disciples entitled, "Hygiene on the Highest: Who Wants a Messy Messiah?" you're feeling tired, so you lay in the back of the boat for a quick nap.

Just as you start to drift off to sleep, your disciple John starts poking your shoulder.

"Hey, Jesus! Those dark clouds over there don't look so good," John says, pointing to a huge, ominous cluster in the sky.

"Thank you, John. That's a sweet little man," you tell him and pinch his puffy little marshmallow cheeks.

"Great! We're gonna die out here," Thomas growls. "I knew it!"

"But those clouds can't hurt us. We're in the water and they're in the air," Philip replies proudly.

Everyone stares at him vacantly for a moment.

"Can I please push Philip overboard?" Thomas asks.

You shrug. Why not?

Just then, lightning crashes, sheets of rain start pouring down, the wind howls, and waves toss the boat around. It's a huge storm, but maybe not bad enough to ruin your nap over.

Philip falls overboard, screaming for help.

"I swear I did not do that!" Thomas yells.

"Help us, Jesus! Before we all perish!" Matthew cries.

You begrudgingly stand up, steady yourself, and take a look around. The crew has lost control of the boat and it seems like at any minute the whole thing will be torn apart or sink.

You've got to do something. Or not. You'll never get back to sleep with all this thunder and lightning going on anyway.

If you walk out onto water to further freak out your disciples, turn to PAGE 16

If you calm the storm with your limitless powers, turn to PAGE 50

If you do nothing and let nature take its course, turn to PAGE 104

158

Thomas' violent distraction worked just like you had planned! Now for a quick getaway!

"Now for a quick getaway!" you exclaim, poking your finger high into the air.

Immediately, six guards seize you and carry you into the city to stand trial before the Governor Pontious Pilate.

"Ah yes, Mr. Christ," he announces. "My men tell me that you tried to escape when they captured you."

"Yes, Your Honor," you meekly answer. "In all fairness, all I did was declare my intentions of a hasty escape...Uh, can I talk to a lawyer?"

"Quiet! One of my men lost an ear during the scuffle of your arrest. That man had a family. What kind of guard can he be now with only one good ear? We had to execute him a few minutes ago, of course, as he was of little use to this city's defense. How does that make you feel?"

"Pretty crummy," you gulp.

"I'm not convinced that our Messiah would do such a cowardly and irresponsible thing. As a matter of fact, I fancy you as just another Messiah wannabe. Henceforth, the scribes will strike your name and all of your alleged miracles from the official scrolls. Furthermore, I do hereby order you to be pulled into quarters by horses and your body parts burned and dragged through the streets. Good day, sir. I said good day."

Within minutes, all of that happens. Afterwards, your spirit ascends to Heaven, but when you get there, the Pearly Gates refuse to open for you. What the heck?

You notice a sign hanging on the gates and give it a read:

THE END

This Spiritual paradise closed to all cowards. Kindly go to Hell, where all cowardly cowards spend eternity for being such stupid cowards.
Signed,
GOD

Days later, your boat pulls into the port of Gadarenes for supplies.

Seconds after you hop ashore to stretch your legs, some local hick pig farmers recognize you as "that Jesus fella" and rush off to tell the rest of the town.

A few minutes later, you see a group of men dragging something bound with a large number of chains and ropes.

It's a naked man, and he struggles and spits and curses like an absolute lunatic.

"He's an absolute lunatic," one of the men tells you. "All filled up with demons. He steals our bread, digs up our graves, and uses adult language around our goats."

"That kind of behavior might be kosher in some communities, but we ain't comfortable with it around these here parts," another farmer adds.

You turn to the possessed man and ask him what his name is.

"We are Legion," he answers in a deep, scary voice. "Because that's how many devils are in here."

"Hey, is a legion more than a million?" asks Philip.

"Maybe it is," the possessed man says.

"Narrr. Actually, a legion is only about six thousand," Andrew says.

"Yeah well, uh, we meant to say we are called Million, not Legion," the possessed man replies. "Because there're so damn many of us demons inside here, we can barely keep track of us all."

He tears at the chains, actually snapping a couple of them.

"At least it's not a billion," Matthew says. "That would be, like, a thousand times worse."

"There are numbers bigger than a billion, you know," James #1 says. "Like seventy times seven."

"Oh yeah," the disciples all say in unison, lost in thought.

"I'm going to kill you and use your empty skulls for chamber pots," the man growls and yanks himself free from more of his trappings.

This is getting out of hand. You strike your favorite demon-rebuking pose.

"Listen up, demons," you begin. "Whether there's two or a dozen or thousands of you in this man, I command you to come out! Shazam!"

The possessed man laughs and snaps more of his chains.

"Uh…sim sala bim! Hocus pocus! Zip zap…zop? Presto chango?"

Turn to the NEXT PAGE

160

Nothing's working. You can't remember the right words!

The pressure's too much. All the farmers are cowering, your disciples are arguing about numbers, and somewhere, a bunch of pigs are oinking. What's with all that oinking anyway?

You turn to one of the pig farmers.

"Can you please shut those pigs up? They're distracting me with all that rooting around and grunting and carrying on and what-not!"

"Them pigs do whatever they wants to do. Can't do nuthin' 'bout it," the farmer says.

Hmm. Maybe the demons need to be transferred into something else. Something like those stupid pigs! Or you could fool the demons into thinking you're also possessed. Maybe then they'll be easier to deal with.

Better decide quick. Those chains won't hold him much longer…

If you cast the demons into the nearby pigs, turn to
PAGE 69

If you trick the demons into thinking you are
possessed, turn to PAGE 73

ABOUT THE AUTHOR

Brock LaBorde is a writing writer man who writes. His first book, <u>The Semi-Complete Guide to Sort of Being a Gentleman</u>, is being developed into a televised TV show for television. This book is his second book. Brock founded and runs Studio8.net, the wildly popular online comedy website on the internet. Sometimes, if you're lucky, you can see him on the television, too. His latest TV project, "The House That Drips Blood on Alex" stars cult film icon Tommy Wiseau and is airing on Comedy Central. Currently, Brock lives in Los Angeles, but that's a secret, ok?